PROFILES
IN COURAGE

PROFILES IN COURAGE

YOUNG READERS MEMORIAL EDITION
Abridged

John F. Kennedy

Special Memorial Foreword
by Robert F. Kennedy

Illustrations by Emil Weiss

HARPER & ROW, PUBLISHERS
NEW YORK, EVANSTON, AND LONDON

The publisher's profits on this Memorial Edition will be used to establish a John F. Kennedy Memorial Award in biography and history (including current history).

Robert F. Kennedy's earnings for the special Foreword will be given to the John F. Kennedy Memorial Library.

PROFILES IN COURAGE—Young Readers Memorial Edition
Foreword copyright © 1964 by Robert F. Kennedy
Copyright © 1955, 1956, 1961 by John F. Kennedy

Harper & Row, Publishers, Incorporated, 49 East 33rd Street, New York 16, N. Y.

Library of Congress catalog card number: 64-17696

B-Q

To My Wife

He well knows what snares are spread about his path, from personal animosity . . . and possibly from popular delusion. But he has put to hazard his ease, his security, his interest, his power, even his . . . popularity . . . He is traduced and abused for his supposed motives. He will remember that obloquy is a necessary ingredient in the composition of all true glory: he will remember . . . that calumny and abuse are essential parts of triumph . . . He may live long, he may do much. But here is the summit. He never can exceed what he does this day.

> Edmund Burke's eulogy of Charles James Fox for his attack upon the tyranny of the East India Company— House of Commons, December 1, 1783

CONTENTS

ILLUSTRATIONS

FOREWORD TO
THE MEMORIAL EDITION

Courage is the virtue that President Kennedy most admired. He sought out those people who had demonstrated in some way, whether it was on a battlefield or a baseball diamond, in a speech or fighting for a cause, that they had courage, that they would stand up, that they could be counted on.

That is why this book so fitted his personality, his beliefs. It is a study of men who, at risk to themselves, their futures, even the well-being of their children, stood fast for principle. It was toward that ideal that he modeled his life. And this in time gave heart to others.

As Andrew Jackson said, "One man with courage makes a majority." That is the effect President Kennedy had on others.

President Kennedy would have been forty-seven in May of 1964. At least one half of the days that he spent on this earth were days of intense physical pain. He had scarlet fever when he was very young, and serious back trouble when he was older. In between he had almost every other conceivable ailment. When we were growing up together we used to laugh about the great risk a mosquito took in biting Jack Kennedy—with some of his blood the mosquito was almost sure to die. He was in Chelsea Naval Hospital for an extended period of time after the war, had a major and painful operation on his back in 1955, campaigned on crutches in 1958. In 1951 on a trip we took around the world he became ill. We flew to the military hospital in Okinawa and he had a temperature of over 106 degrees. They didn't think he would live.

But during all this time, I never heard him complain. I never heard him say anything that would indicate that he felt God had dealt with him unjustly. Those who knew him well would know he was suffering only because his face was a little whiter, the lines around his eyes were a little deeper, his words a little sharper. Those who did not know him well detected nothing.

He didn't complain about his problem, so why should I complain about mine—that is how one always felt.

When he battled against illness, when he fought in the war, when he ran for the Senate, when he stood up against powerful interests in Massachusetts to fight for the St. Lawrence Seaway, when he fought for a labor reform act in 1959, when he entered the West Virginia primary in 1960, when he debated Lyndon Johnson at the Democratic Convention in Los Angeles with no advance notice, when he took the blame completely on himself for the failure at the Bay of Pigs, when he fought the steel companies, when he stood up at Berlin in 1961 and then again in 1962 for the freedom of that city, when he forced the withdrawal of the Soviet missiles from Cuba, when he spoke and fought for equal rights for all our citizens, and hundreds of other things both big and small, he was reflecting what is the best in the human being.

He was demonstrating conviction, courage, a desire to help others who needed help, and true and genuine love for his country.

Because of his efforts, the mentally retarded and the mentally ill will have a better chance, the young a greater opportunity to be educated and live with dignity and self-respect, the ill to be cared for, the world to live in peace.

President Kennedy had only a thousand days in the White House instead of three thousand days, yet so much was accomplished. Still so much needs to be done.

This book tells the stories of men who in their own time recognized what needed to be done—and did it. President Kennedy was fond of quoting Dante that "the hottest places in Hell are reserved for those who, in a time of great moral crisis, maintain their neutrality."

If there is a lesson from the lives of the men John Kennedy depicts in this book, if there is a lesson from his life and from his death, it is that in this world of ours none of us can afford to be lookers-on, the critics standing on the sidelines.

Thomas Carlyle wrote, "The courage we desire and prize is not the courage to die decently but to live manfully."

On the morning of his death, President Kennedy called former Vice President John Nance Garner to pay his respects. It was Mr. Garner's ninety-fifth birthday. When Mr. Garner first came to Washington the total federal budget was less than 500 million dollars. President Kennedy was administering a budget of just under 100 billion dollars.

President Kennedy's grandmother was living in Boston when President Kennedy was assassinated. She was also alive the year President Lincoln was shot.

We are a young country. We are growing and expanding until it appears that this planet will no longer contain us. We have problems now that people fifty, even ten years ago, would not have dreamed would have to be faced.

The energies and talents of all of us are needed to meet the challenges—the internal ones of our cities, our farms, ourselves—to be successful in the fight for freedom around the globe, in the battles against illiteracy, hunger and disease. Pleasantries, self-satisfied mediocrity will serve us badly. We need the best of many—not of just a few. We must strive for excellence.

Lord Tweedsmuir, one of the President's favorite authors, wrote in his autobiography: "Public life is the crown of a career, and to young men it is the worthiest ambition. Politics is still the greatest and most honorable adventure."

It has been fashionable in many places to look down on politics, on those in Government. President Kennedy, I think, changed that and altered the public conception of Government. He certainly did for those who participated. But, however we feel about politics, the arena of Government is where the decisions will be made which will affect not only all our destinies but the future of our children born and unborn.

At the time of the Cuban missile crisis last year, we discussed the possibility of war, a nuclear exchange, and talked about being killed—the latter at that time seemed so unimportant, almost frivolous. The one matter which really was of concern to him and truly had meaning and made that time much more fearful than it would otherwise have been was the specter of the death of the children of this country and around the world—the young people who had no part and knew nothing of the confrontation, but whose lives would be snuffed out like everyone else's. They would never have been given a chance to make a decision, to vote in an election, to run for office, to lead a revolution, to determine their own destinies.

We, our generation, had. And the great tragedy was that if we erred, we erred not just for ourselves, our futures, our homes, our country, but for the lives, futures, homes and countries of those who never had been given an opportunity to play a role, to vote "aye" or "nay," to make themselves felt.

Bonar Law said, "There is no such thing as inevitable war. If war comes it will be from failure of human wisdom."

It is true. It is human wisdom that is needed not just on our side but on all sides. I might add that if wisdom had not been demonstrated by the American President and also by Premier Khrushchev, then the world as we know it would have been destroyed.

But there will be future Cubas. There will be future crises. We have the problems of the hungry, the neglected, the poor and the downtrodden. They must receive more help. And just as solutions had to be found in October of 1962, answers must be found for these other problems that still face us. So that wisdom is needed still.

John Quincy Adams, Daniel Webster, Sam Houston, Thomas Hart Benton, Edmund G. Ross, Lucius Quintus Cincinnatus Lamar, George Norris and Robert Taft imparted a heritage to us. They came, they left their mark, and this country was not the same because these men had lived. By how much the good of what they did and deeded to us was cherished, nurtured and encouraged, by so much did the country and all of us gain.

And so it is also for John F. Kennedy. Like these others, his life had an import, meant something to the country while he was alive. More significant, however, is what we do with what is left, with what has been started. It was his conviction, like Plato's, that the definition of citizenship in a democracy is participation in Government and that, as Francis Bacon wrote, it is "left only to God and to the angels to be lookers on." It was his conviction that a democracy with this effort by its people must and can face its problems, that it must show patience, restraint, compassion, as well as wisdom and strength and courage, in the struggle for solutions which are very rarely easy to find.

It was his conviction that we should do so successfully because the courage of those who went before us in this land exists in the present generation of Americans.

"We dare not forget today that we are the heirs of that first revolution. Let the word go forth from this time and place, to friend and foe alike, that the torch has been passed to a new generation of Americans—born in this century, tempered by war, disciplined by a hard and bitter peace, proud of our ancient heritage—and unwilling to witness or permit the slow undoing of those human rights to which this nation has always been committed, and to which we are committed today at home and around the world."

This book is not just the stories of the past but a book of hope and confidence for the future. What happens to the country, to the world, depends on what we do with what others have left us.

—ROBERT F. KENNEDY

December 18, 1963

PREFACE

Since first reading—long before I entered the Senate—
an account of John Quincy Adams and his struggle with
the Federalist party, I have been interested in the problems of political courage in the face of constituent pressures, and the light shed on those problems by the lives
of past statesmen. A long period of hospitalization and
convalescence following a spinal operation in October,
1954, gave me my first opportunity to do the reading and
research necessary for this project.

I am not a professional historian; and, although all
errors of fact and judgment are exclusively my own, I
should like to acknowledge with sincere gratitude those
who assisted me in the preparation of this volume. The
entire manuscript was greatly improved by the criticisms
of Professor Allan Nevins of Columbia University, one
of the foremost political historians and biographers of
our times.

I owe a special debt of gratitude to an outstanding
American institution—the Library of Congress. Throughout the many months of my absence from Washington,
the Legislative Reference and Loan Divisions of the Library fulfilled all of my requests for books with amazing

promptness and cheerful courtesy. Dr. George Galloway,
and particularly Dr. William R. Tansill, of the Library
Staff, made important contributions to the selection of
examples for inclusion in the book, as did Arthur Krock
of the *New York Times* and Professor James McGregor
Burns of Williams College.

Professor John Bystrom of the University of Minnesota,
former Nebraska Attorney General C. A. Sorensen, and
the Honorable Hugo Srb, Clerk of the Nebraska State
Legislature, were helpful in providing previously un-
published correspondence of George Norris and pertinent
documents of the Nebraska State Legislature.

Professor Jules Davids of Georgetown University assisted materially in the preparation of several chapters,
as did my able friend James M. Landis, who delights in
bringing the precision of the lawyer to the mysteries of
history.

Chapters 1 through 8 were greatly improved by the
criticisms of Professors Arthur N. Holcombe and Arthur
M. Schlesinger, Jr., both of Harvard; and Professor Walter Johnson of the University of Chicago. The editorial
suggestions, understanding cooperation and initial encouragement which I received from Evan Thomas of
Harper & Brothers made this book possible.

To Gloria Liftman and Jane Donovan, my thanks for
their efforts above and beyond the call of duty in typing
and retyping this manuscript.

The greatest debt is owed to my research associate,
Theodore C. Sorensen, for his invaluable assistance in the
assembly and preparation of the material upon which this
book is based.

This book would not have been possible without the encouragement, assistance and criticisms offered from the very beginning by my wife Jacqueline, whose help during all the days of my convalescence I cannot ever adequately acknowledge.

—JOHN F. KENNEDY

Dear Young Reader:

This is largely a book about politicians who were failures.

Most were deprived of any hope of achieving their most cherished goals in public life. Many were rejected by the people and forced to live in obscurity away from the political arena which they enjoyed so much.

But what is important about these men is not their failures, but why they failed—not the goals they did not reach, but what kept them from these goals. Each of them had some principle or idea which he believed in; and when the time came, each of them chose to act according to his beliefs even though to do so meant unpopularity and criticism and often defeat in elections.

That is why this book is called *Profiles in Courage.* For it takes great courage to do what you think is right even though it may mean the end of your career and the dislike and criticism of your friends and neighbors. Many people never have the opportunity to show such courage. But all of us have the opportunity to recognize such courage in others, to respect the person who is doing what he believes to be right even though we think he is wrong.

That is why this book is more than an exciting story of great men. It is a lesson to all of us that courage is much more than bravery on a battlefield; that it can mean acting according to your beliefs whatever the consequences. And it is also a lesson that we can all share in such courage by refusing to join with those people who make unreasoning attacks on the man who is doing or saying what he honestly believes to be right.

COURAGE AND POLITICS

THIS IS A BOOK about that most admirable of human virtues—courage. "Grace under pressure," Ernest Hemingway defined it. And these are the stories of the pressures experienced by eight United States Senators and the grace with which they endured them—the risks to their careers, the unpopularity of their courses, the defamation of their characters, and sometimes, but sadly only sometimes, the vindication of their reputations and their principles.

A nation which has forgotten the quality of courage which in the past has been brought to public life is not as likely to insist upon or reward that quality in its chosen leaders today—and in fact we have forgotten. We may remember how John Quincy Adams became President through the political schemes of Henry Clay, but we have forgotten how, as a young man, he gave up a promising Senatorial career to stand by the nation. We may remember Daniel Webster for his subservience to the National Bank throughout much of his career, but we have forgotten his sacrifice for the national good at the close of that career. We do not remember—and possibly we do not care.

Walter Lippmann, after nearly half a century of careful observation, rendered in his recent book a harsh judgment both on the politician and the electorate:

> With exceptions so rare they are regarded as miracles of nature, successful democratic politicians are insecure and intimidated men. They advance politically only as they placate, appease, bribe, seduce, bamboozle, or otherwise manage to manipulate the demanding threatening elements in their constituencies. The decisive consideration is not whether the proposition is good but whether it is popular—not whether it will work well and prove itself, but whether the active-talking constituents like it immediately.

I am not so sure, after years of living and working in the midst of "successful democratic politicians," that they are all "insecure and intimidated men." I am convinced that the complication of public business and the competition for the public's attention have obscured innumerable acts of political courage—large and small—performed almost daily in the Senate Chamber. I am convinced that the decline—if there has been a decline—has been less in the Senate than in the public's appreciation of the art of politics, of the nature and necessity for compromise and balance, and of the nature of the Senate as a legislative chamber. And, finally, I am convinced that we have criticized those who have followed the crowd—and at the same time criticized those who have defied it

—because we have not fully understood the responsibility of a Senator to his constituents or recognized the difficulty facing a politician conscientiously desiring, in Webster's words, "to push [his] skiff from the shore alone" into a hostile and turbulent sea. Perhaps if the American people more fully comprehended the terrible pressures which discourage acts of political courage, which drive a Senator to abandon or subdue his conscience, then they might be less critical of those who take the easier road—and more appreciative of those still able to follow the path of courage.

The *first* pressure to be mentioned is a form of pressure rarely recognized by the general public. Americans want to be liked—and Senators are no exception. They are by nature—and of necessity—social animals. We enjoy the comradeship and approval of our friends and colleagues. We prefer praise to abuse, popularity to contempt. Realizing that the path of the conscientious insurgent must frequently be a lonely one, we are anxious to get along with our fellow legislators, our fellow members of the club, to abide by the clubhouse rules and patterns, not to pursue a unique and independent course which would embarrass or irritate the other members. We realize, moreover, that our influence in the club—and the extent to which we can accomplish our objectives and those of our constituents—are dependent in some measure on the esteem with which we are regarded by other Senators.

It is thinking of that next campaign—the desire to be re-elected—that provides the *second* pressure on the conscientious Senator. It should not automatically be assumed that this is a wholly selfish motive—although it is not unnatural that those who have chosen politics as their profession should seek to continue their careers—for Senators who go down to defeat in a vain defense of a single principle will not be on hand to fight for that or any other principle in the future.

The *third* and most significant source of pressures which discourage political courage in the conscientious Senator or Congressman—and practically all of the problems described in this chapter apply equally to members of both Houses—is the pressure of his constituency, the interest groups, the organized letter writers, the economic blocs and even the average voter. To cope with such pressures, to defy them or even to satisfy them, is a formidable task. All of us occasionally have the urge to follow the example of Congressman John Steven McGroarty of California, who wrote a constituent in 1934:

> One of the countless drawbacks of being in Congress is that I am compelled to receive impertinent letters from a jackass like you in which you say I promised to have the Sierra Madre mountains reforested and I have been in Congress two months and haven't done it. Will you please take two running jumps and go to hell.

Fortunately or unfortunately, few follow that urge—but the provocation is there—not only from unreasonable letters and impossible requests, but also from hopelessly inconsistent demands and endlessly unsatisfied grievances.

These, then, are some of the pressures which confront a man of conscience. He cannot ignore the pressure groups, his constituents, his party, the comradeship of his colleagues, the needs of his family, his own pride in office, the necessity for compromise and the importance of remaining in office. He must judge for himself which path to choose, which step will most help or hinder the ideals to which he is committed. He realizes that once he begins to weigh each issue in terms of his chances for re-election, once he begins to compromise away his principles on one issue after another for fear that to do otherwise would halt his career and prevent future fights for principle, then he has lost the very freedom of conscience which justifies his continuance in office. But to decide at which point and on which issue he will risk his career is a difficult and soul-searching decision.

Today the challenge of political courage looms larger than ever before. For our everyday life is becoming so saturated with the tremendous power of mass communications that any unpopular or unorthodox course arouses a storm of protests such as John Quincy Adams—under attack in 1807—could never have envisioned. Our political life is becoming so expensive, so mechanized and so dominated by professional politicians and public relations men that the idealist who dreams of independent statesmanship is rudely awakened by the necessities of election and accomplishment.

And thus, in the days ahead, only the very courageous will be able to take the hard and unpopular decisions

necessary for our survival in the struggle with a powerful
enemy—an enemy with leaders who need give little
thought to the popularity of their course, who need pay
little tribute to the public opinion they themselves ma-
nipulate, and who may force, without fear of retaliation
at the polls, their citizens to sacrifice present laughter for
future glory. And only the very courageous will be able
to keep alive the spirit of individualism and dissent which
gave birth to this nation, nourished it as an infant and
carried it through its severest tests upon the attainment
of its maturity.

We shall need compromises in the days ahead, to be
sure. But these will be, or should be, compromises of
issues, not of principles. Compromise need not mean
cowardice. Indeed it is frequently the compromisers and
conciliators who are faced with the severest tests of political courage as they oppose the extremist views of their
constituents. It was because Daniel Webster conscientiously favored compromise in 1850 that he earned a
condemnation unsurpassed in the annals of political history.

His is a story worth remembering today. So, I believe,
are the stories of other Senators of courage—men whose
abiding loyalty to their nation triumphed over all personal and political considerations, men who showed the
real meaning of courage and a real faith in democracy,
men who made the Senate of the United States something more than a mere collection of robots dutifully recording the views of their constituents, or a gathering of
time-servers skilled only in predicting and following the
tides of public sentiment.

Whatever their differences, the American politicians whose stories are here retold shared that one heroic quality—courage. In the pages that follow, I have attempted to set forth their lives—the ideals they lived for and the principles they fought for, their virtues and their sins, their dreams and their disillusionments, the praise they earned and the abuse they endured. All this may be set down on the printed page. It is ours to write about, it is ours to read about. But there was in the lives of each of these men something that it is difficult for the printed page to capture—and yet something that has reached the homes and enriched the heritage of every citizen in every part of the land.

PROFILES
IN COURAGE

PART ONE

THE TIME AND THE PLACE

THE ORIGINAL twenty-two United States Senators, meeting in New York in 1789, at first seemed to fulfill the expectations of the makers of the Constitution. A distinguished and glittering gathering of eminent and experienced statesmen, the Senate, as compared with the House of Representatives, was on the whole far more pompous and formal, its chambers far more elaborate, and its members far more concerned with elegance of dress and social rank. Meeting behind closed doors, without the use of standing committees, the Senate consulted personally with President Washington, and acted very nearly as an integral part of the administration.

But, as it must to all legislative bodies, politics came to the United States Senate. As the Federalist party split on foreign policy and Thomas Jefferson resigned from the Cabinet to organize his followers, the Senate became a forum for criticism of the executive branch, and the role of executive council was assumed instead by a Cabinet of men upon whom the President could depend to share his views and be responsible to him.

Gradually the Senate assumed more of the aspects of a

legislative body. In 1794 public galleries were authorized for regular legislative sessions; in 1801 newspaper correspondents were admitted; and by 1803 the Senate was debating who should have the privilege of coming upon the Senate floor. Congressmen, Ambassadors, Department Heads and Governors could be agreed upon, but what about "the ladies"? Senator Wright contended "that their presence gives a pleasing and necessary animation to debate, polishing the speakers' arguments and softening their manner." But John Quincy Adams, whose puritanical candor on such occasions will be subsequently noted, replied that the ladies "introduced noise and confusion into the Senate, and debates were protracted to arrest their attention." (The motion to admit "the ladies" was defeated 16-12, although this policy of exclusion would be reversed in later years, only to be restored in modern times.)

Although Senators were paid the munificent sum of $6 per day, and their privileges included the use of great silver snuffboxes on the Senate floor, the aristocratic manners which had characterized the first Senate were strangely out of place when the struggling hamlet of Washington became the capital city in 1800, for its rugged surroundings contrasted sharply with those enjoyed at the temporary capitals in New York and Philadelphia. Formality in Senate procedures was retained, however—although Vice President Aaron Burr, himself an object of some disrepute after killing Hamilton in a duel, frequently found it necessary to call Senators to order for "eating apples and cakes in their seats" and walking between those engaged in discussion.

Nevertheless, the House, still small enough to be a truly deliberative body, overshadowed the Senate in terms of political power during the first three decades of our government. Madison said that "being a young man and desirous of increasing his reputation as a statesman, he could not afford to accept a seat in the Senate," whose debates had little influence on public opinion.

It was a time of change—in the Senate, in the concept of our government, in the growth of the two-party system, in the spread of democracy to the farm and the frontier and in the United States of America. Men who were flexible, men who could move with or ride over the changing currents of public opinion, men who sought their glory in the dignity of the Senate rather than its legislative accomplishments—these were the men for such times. But young John Quincy Adams of Massachusetts was not such a man.

JOHN QUINCY ADAMS

"The magistrate is the servant
not . . . of the people but of his God."

THE YOUNG SENATOR from Massachusetts stirred restlessly in his chair as the debate droned on. The half-filled Senate chamber fairly echoed with the shouting of his Massachusetts colleague, Senator Pickering, who was denouncing President Jefferson's Trade Embargo of 1807 for what seemed like the one hundreth time. Outside, a dreary January rain had bogged the dismal village of Washington in a sea of mud. Sorting the mail from Massachusetts which lay in disarray on his desk, John Quincy Adams found his eye caught by an unfamiliar handwriting, on an envelope with no return address. Inside was a single sheet of fine linen paper, and the Senator grimly read its anonymous message a second time before crumpling letter and envelope into the basket by his desk:

Lucifer, Son of the Morning, how thou hast fallen! We hope not irrecoverably. Oh Adams, remember who thou art. Return to Massachusetts! Return to

thy country. Assist not in its destruction! Consider
the consequences! Awake—arouse in time!

A FEDERALIST

A Federalist! Adams mused bitterly over the
word. Was he not the son of the last Federalist
President? Had he not served Federalist administrations in the diplomatic service abroad? Had
he not been elected as a Federalist to the Massachusetts Legislature and then to the United
States Senate? Now, simply because he had
placed national interest before party and section,
the Federalists had deserted him. Yes, he thought,
I did not desert them, as they charge—it is they
who have deserted me.

> My political prospects are declining [he wrote in
> his diary that night] and as my term of service draws
> near its close, I am constantly approaching to the
> certainty of being restored to the situation of a pri-
> vate citizen. For this event, however, I hope to have
> my mind sufficiently prepared. In the meantime, I
> implore that Spirit from whom every good and per-
> fect gift descends to enable me to render essential
> service to my country, and that I may never be
> governed in my public conduct by any consideration
> other than that of my duty.

These are not merely the sentiments of a courageous Senator, they are also the words of a Puritan

statesman. For John Quincy Adams was one of the great representatives of that extraordinary breed who have left a memorable imprint upon our Government and our way of life. Harsh and intractable, like the rocky New England countryside which colored his attitude toward the world at large, the Puritan gave meaning, consistency and character to the early days of the American Republic. His somber sense of responsibility toward his Creator he carried into every phase of his daily life. He believed that man was made in the image of God, and thus he believed him equal to the extraordinary demands of self-government. The Puritan loved liberty and he loved the law; he had a genius for determining the precise point where the rights of the state and the rights of the individual could be reconciled.

In John Quincy Adams these very characteristics were unhappily out of tune with the party intrigues and political passions of the day. Long before those discouraging months in the Senate when his mail was filled with abuse from the Massachusetts Federalists, long before he had even entered the Senate, he had noted in his diary the dangers that confronted a Puritan entering politics: "I feel strong temptation to plunge into political controversy," he had written, "but . . . a politician in this country must be the man of a party. I would fain be the man of my whole country."

Few if any Americans have been born with the advantages of John Quincy Adams: a famous name; a brilliant father who labored unceasingly to develop his son's natural talents; and an extraordinary mother. Indeed he was born with everything to make for a happy and successful life except for those qualities that bring peace of mind. In spite of a life of extraordinary achievement, he was gnawed constantly by a sense of inadequacy, of frustration, of failure. Though his hard New England conscience and his remarkable talents drove him steadily along a road of unparalleled success, he had from the beginning an almost morbid sense of constant failure.

Yet the lifetime which was so bitterly deprecated by its own principal has never been paralleled in American history. John Quincy Adams— until his death at eighty in the Capitol—held more important offices and participated in more important events than anyone in the history of our nation, as Minister to The Hague, Emissary to England, Minister to Prussia, State Senator, United States Senator, Minister to Russia, Head of the American Mission to negotiate peace with England, Minister to England, Secretary of State,

President of the United States and member of the House of Representatives. He figured, in one capacity or another, in the American Revolution, the War of 1812 and the prelude to the Civil War. Among the acquaintances and colleagues who march across the pages of his diary are Sam Adams (a kinsman), John Hancock, Washington, Jefferson, Franklin, Lafayette, John Jay, James Madison, James Monroe, John Marshall, Henry Clay, Andrew Jackson, Thomas Hart Benton, John Tyler, John C. Calhoun, Daniel Webster, Lincoln, James Buchanan, William Lloyd Garrison, Andrew Johnson, Jefferson Davis and many others.

It was not unnatural that John Quincy, returning to Boston after diplomatic service abroad upon his father's defeat for President by Thomas Jefferson, should become active in the affairs of his father's party. He admired the Federalists as the founders of the Constitution, the champions of naval power and a bulwark against French Revolutionary influences.

But no sooner had the young ex-diplomat been elected as a Federalist to the Massachusetts legislature when he demonstrated his audacious disdain for narrow partisanship. Without consulting his senior colleagues, he proposed—only forty-eight hours after he had become a member of that august

legislative body—that the Republican (Jefferso-
nian or Democratic) party be given proportional
representation on the Governor's council. (Adams
later noted that this act of nonpartisan independence "marked the principle by which my whole
public life has been governed from that day to
this.")

In subsequently selecting young Adams for the
Senate, his colleagues in the state legislature may
have assumed that the honor for one of his com-
parative youth would help impress upon him his
obligations to his party.

Arriving in Washington, Adams promptly indicated his disregard for both party affiliations and
customary freshman reticence. Although illness in
the family had prevented him from arriving in
time to vote on ratification of President Jefferson's
treaty for the purchase of the Louisiana Territory,
he promptly aroused a storm of controversy by becoming the only Federalist to support that prece-
dent-shattering acquisition actively on the floor
and to vote for an $11 million appropriation to
effectuate it. His democratic principles also caused
him to fight administration measures for imposing
a government and taxes upon the residents of the
Territory—thus incurring the opposition of his Re-

publican colleagues as well. But, with a vision of an American stretched to its continental limits, he regarded Jefferson's remarkable feat in excluding Napoleon from our boundaries while enriching our nation as far more important than the outraged astonishment of his Federalist colleagues. Concerned primarily with maintaining the hegemony of New England, they feared westward expansion would diminish the political and economic influence of the commercial cities of the Northeast, lower the value of Eastern lands in which they were financially interested, and provide the Jeffersonians with a permanent majority in Congress. The young Federalist from Massachusetts, as though he were oblivious to their attitude, heaped fuel upon the fires of Federalist rage by attending a banquet of Jeffersonians in celebration of the purchase!

The possession of the proud name of Adams could not prevent—and may well have hastened—the young Senator's gradual emergence as a minority of one. Had his political philosophy been more popular, his personal mannerisms would still have made close alliances difficult. He was, after all, "an Adams . . . cold, tactless and rigidly conscientious." The son of an unpopular father, a renegade in his

party and rather brash for a freshman Senator,
John Quincy neither sought nor was offered political alliances or influence.

But if the Federalist party learned to dislike the
"stripling" even more intensely than they had disliked "his sire," it must be said that any Federalist
love for John Quincy would have been wasted
anyway. For he became increasingly contemptuous of the Federalist party. An American nationalist who had lived a great part of his brief life
abroad, he could not yield his devotion to the national interest for the narrowly partisan, parochial
and pro-British outlook which dominated New
England's first political party. His former colleagues in the State Legislature publicly charged
him with ungrateful "conduct worthy of Machia-
velli"; but he wrote his mother that he felt that, as
Senator, he could best determine what Massachusetts' best interests were, and "if Federalism con-
sists in looking to the British navy as the only
palladium of our liberty, I must be a political
heretic."

Many Senators before and after 1804 have com-
batted the ill-effects of being termed a political
heretic by their party chieftains by building strong
personal popularity among their constituents. This
became increasingly possible as universal man-

hood suffrage became general early in the nineteenth century. But not John Quincy Adams. He regarded every public measure that came before him, a fellow Senator observed, as though it were an abstract proposition from Euclid, unfettered by considerations of political appeal. His guiding star was the principle of Puritan statesmanship his father had laid down many years before: *"The magistrate is the servant not of his own desires, not even of the people, but of his God."*

But it was not until 1807 that the split between party and Senator became irreparable, and Adams was denounced by the great majority of his constituents, as well as the party chiefs. The final break, naturally enough, concerned this nation's foreign policy. As our relations with Great Britain worsened, our ships were seized, our cargoes were confiscated, and our seamen were "impressed" by British cruisers and compelled to serve—as alleged British subjects—in the King's navy. Thousands of American seamen were taken on an organized basis, ships were lost at sea for want of men, and even those able to "prove" American citizenship were frequently refused permission to return. Adams' patriotic instincts were aroused, and he was indignant that the very Federalist merchants whose ships were attacked had decided that appeasement of Great Britain was the only answer to their problems. His Federalist colleagues even attempted to rationalize such aggressive measures by talking vaguely of Britain's difficulties in her war with France and our friendly tone toward the latter. With undisguised contempt for this attitude, Adams in 1806 had introduced and pushed to passage—successfully—a unique experience for him, he noted in his diary—a series of resolutions condemning British aggressions upon American ships, and requesting the President to demand restoration and indemnification of the confiscated vessels. The Federalists, of course, had solidly opposed his measures, as they did an Adams-supported administration bill limiting British imports. He was now, for all practical purposes, a man without a party.

Finally, in the summer of 1807, the American frigate *Chesapeake* was summarily fired upon off the Virginia Capes by the British man-of-war *Leopard*, after the American vessel had refused either to be searched or to hand over four seamen whom the English claimed to be British subjects. Several of the American crew were killed or injured. The incensed Adams was convinced that, party or no party, the time for forceful action against such intolerable acts had come. He pleaded

The Leopard *fires upon the* Chesapeake.

with local Federalist officials to call a town meeting in Boston to protest the incident. Turned down, and outraged when a prominent Federalist attempted to justify even the *Leopard*'s attack, he discovered to his grim satisfaction that the Republican party was organizing a similar mass meeting to be held at the State House that very week.

The Federalist *Repertory* warned the faithful that the meeting represented nothing but an "irregular and tumultuous mode of proceeding," which "no just or honorable man" should attend. But John Quincy Adams did attend; and, although he declined to serve as moderator, he nevertheless was instrumental in drafting the group's fighting resolution which pledged to the President the lives and fortunes of the participants in support of "any measures, however serious."

Now the Federalists were outraged. Although they hurriedly called an official town meeting to pledge hypocritically their support to the President too, they stated publicly that John Quincy Adams, for his public association with Republican meetings and causes, should "have his head taken off for apostasy . . . and should no longer be considered as having any communion with the party." It was this episode, the Senator later commented, "which alienated me from that day and forever from the councils of the Federalist party."

When Jefferson on September 18, 1807, called upon Congress to retaliate against the British by enacting an embargo effectively shutting off all further international trade—a measure apparently ruinous to Massachusetts, the leading commercial state in the nation—it was John Quincy Adams of Massachusetts who rose on the Senate floor and called for referral of the message to a select committee; who was appointed Chairman of the committee; and who reported both the Embargo Bill and a bill of his own preventing British vessels from entering American waters.

"This measure will cost you and me our seats," young Adams remarked to a colleague, as the select committee completed its work and its members made their way to the Senate floor, "but private interest must not be put in opposition to public good."

The Federalist leaders insisted the Embargo was an attempt by Jefferson to ruin New England prosperity, to provoke England to war, and to aid the French. Even though New England Republicans refused to defend their President's bill, the Federalist party, scoring heavily on the issue, returned triumphantly to power in both Houses of the Massachusetts legislature. Talk of New England seceding became commonplace.

But however great their hatred for Jefferson and his Embargo, Massachusetts Federalists, merchants and other citizens were even more bitter over the "desertion" of their Senator to the ranks of the enemy. "A party scavenger!" snorted the Northampton *Hampshire Gazette*, "one of those ambitious politicians who lives on both land and water, and occasionally resorts to each, but who finally settles down in the mud." Adams, said the Salem *Gazette*, is "a popularity seeker . . . courting the prevailing party," and one of "Bonaparte's Senators." The Greenfield *Gazette* called him an apostate "associated with the assassins of his father's character." His own social circles in Boston —the rich, the cultivated and the influential—all turned against him. "I would not sit at the same table with that renegade," retorted one of Boston's leading citizens in refusing to attend a dinner at which Adams would be present. And a leading Federalist wrote with glee to the Washington party stalwarts, "He walks into State Street at the usual hour but seems totally unknown."

The Federalist Legislature convened at the end of May 1808, with—as the Massachusetts Republican Governor wrote Jefferson—but one "principal object—the political and even the personal destruction of John Quincy Adams." As soon as both Houses had organized, the legislature immediately elected Adams' successor—nine months prior to the expiration of his term! And as its next order of business, the legislature promptly passed resolutions instructing its Senators to urge repeal of the Embargo.

"The election," Adams realized, "was precipitated for the sole purpose of specially marking me. For it ought, in regular order, not to have been made until the winter session of the legislature." And the resolutions, he felt, enjoined "upon their Senators a course of conduct which neither my judgment could approve nor my spirit brook."

Only one course was conscientiously open to him—he resigned his seat in the Senate in order to defend the policies of the man who had driven his father from the Presidency.

It was "out of the question," he wrote, to hold seat "without exercising the most perfect freedom of agency, under the sole and exclusive control of my own sense of right."

> I will only add, that, far from regretting any one of those acts for which I have suffered, I would do them over again, were they now to be done, at the hazard

of ten times as much slander, unpopularity, and displacement.

Hated by the Federalists and suspected by the Republicans, John Quincy Adams returned to private life. His star was soon to rise again; but he never forgot this incident or abandoned his courage of conscience. (Legend has it that during Adams' politically independent term as President, in response to the Presidential toast "May he strike confusion to his foes!" Daniel Webster dryly commented, "As he has already done to his friends.") Soon after his retirement from the White House in 1829, Adams was asked by the voters of the Plymouth District to represent them in Congress. In disregard of the advice of his family and friends and his own desire for leisure time to write his father's biography, he agreed to accept the post if elected. But he specified, first, that he should never be expected to promote himself as a candidate and ask for votes; and, secondly, that he would pursue a course in Congress completely independent of the party and people who elected him. On this basis Adams was elected by an overwhelming vote, and served in the House until his death. Here he wrote perhaps the brightest chapter of his history, for as "Old Man Eloquent" he devoted his remarkable prestige and tireless energies to the struggle against slavery.

To be returned on this independent basis to the Congress from which he had departed so ignominiously twenty-two years earlier was a deeply moving experience for the courageous ex-Senator. "I am a member-elect of the Twenty-Second Congress," he recorded with pride in his diary. "No election or appointment conferred upon me ever gave me so much pleasure. My election as President of the United States was not half so gratifying to my inmost soul."

PART TWO

THE TIME AND THE PLACE

GREAT CRISES produce great men, and great deeds of courage. This country has known no greater crisis than that which culminated in the fratricidal war between North and South in 1861. Thus, without intending to slight other periods of American history, no work of this nature could overlook three acts of outstanding political courage—of vital importance to the eventual maintenance of the Union—which occurred in the fateful decade before the Civil War. In two cases—involving Senators Sam Houston of Texas and Thomas Hart Benton of Missouri, both of whom had enjoyed political dominion in their states for many years—defeat was their reward. In the third—that involving Daniel Webster of Massachusetts—even death, which came within two years of his great decision, did not halt the calumnies heaped upon him by his enemies who had sadly embittered his last days.

It is not surprising that this ten-year period of recurring crises, when the ties that bound the Union were successively snapping, should have brought forth the best, as it did the worst, in our political leaders. All in a position of responsibility were obliged to decide between maintaining their loyalty to the nation or to their state and region. For many on both sides—the abolitionists in the North, the fire-eaters in the South, men who were wholly convinced of the rightness of their section's cause—the decision came easily.

But to those who felt a dual loyalty to their state and their country, to those who sought compromises which would postpone or remove entirely the shadow of war which hung over them, the decision was agonizing, for the ultimate choice involved the breaking of old loyalties and friendships, and the prospect of humiliating political defeat.

The cockpit in which this struggle between North and South was fought was the chamber of the United States Senate. The South, faced with the steadily growing population of the North as reflected in increasing majorities in the House of Representatives, realized that its sole hope of maintaining its power and prestige lay in the Senate. It was for this reason that the admission of new states into the Union, which threatened continuously to upset the precarious balance of power between the free and the slave states, between the agricultural and manufacturing regions, was at the heart of some of the great Senate debates in the first half of the nineteenth century.

In 1820 a law was passed to admit Maine and Missouri into the Union together, one free, the other slave, as part of Henry Clay's first great compromise. In 1836 and 1837, Arkansas and Michigan, and in 1845 and 1846, Florida and Iowa, were admitted through legislation which coupled them together. But the seams of compromise were bursting by 1850, as vast new territories acquired by the Mexican War accelerated the pace of the slavery controversy. The attention of the nation was focused on the Senate, and focused especially on the three most gifted parliamentary leaders in American history— Clay, Calhoun and Webster. Of these, only Daniel Webster was to share with Benton and Houston the ignominy of constituent wrath and the humiliation of political downfall at the hands of the states they had loved and championed. We shall note well the courage of Webster, Benton and Houston; but if we are to understand the times that made their feats heroic, we must first note the leadership of the two Senate giants who formed with Webster the most outstanding triumvirate the Senate has ever known, Henry Clay and John C. Calhoun.

Henry Clay of Kentucky—bold, autocratic and magnetic, fiery in manner with a charm so compelling that an opponent once declined a meeting which would subject him to the appeal of Harry of the West. To Abraham Lincoln, "He was my beau ideal"; to the half-mad, half-genius John Randolph of Roanoke, he was, in what is perhaps the most memorable and malignant sentence in the history of personal abuse, "a being, so brilliant yet so corrupt, which, like a rotten mackerel by moonlight, shines and stinks." Not even John Calhoun, who had fought him for years, was impervious to his fascination: "I don't like Henry Clay. He is a bad man, an impostor, a creator of wicked schemes. I wouldn't speak to him, but, by God, I love him."

Others beside John Calhoun loved him. Like Charles James Fox, he reveled in a love for life, and had a matchless gift for winning and holding the hearts of his fellow-countrymen—and women. Elected to the Senate when still below the constitutional age of thirty, he was subsequently sent to the House where in a move never duplicated before or since he was immediately elected Speaker at the age of thirty-five.

Though he lacked the intellectual resources of Webster and Calhoun, Henry Clay nevertheless had visions of a greater America beyond those held by either of his famous colleagues. And so, in 1820, 1833 and 1850 he initiated, hammered and charmed through reluctant Congresses the three great compromises that preserved the Union until 1861, by which time the strength of the North was such that secession was doomed to failure.

The second and probably the most extraordinary of the triumvirate was John C. Calhoun of South Carolina, with bristling hair and eyes that burned like heavy coals, "the cast-iron man," according to the English spinster, Harriet Martineau, "who looks as if he had never been born, and never could be extinguished." Calhoun, in spite of this appearance, had been born—in 1782, the same year as Webster and five years after Clay. He was six feet, two inches tall; a graduate of Yale University; a Member of Congress at the age of twenty-nine; a War Hawk who joined Henry Clay in driving the United States into the War of 1812; a nationalist who turned sectionalist in the 1820's as the economic pressures of the tariff began to tell on the agricultural economy of South Carolina. Calhoun had a mind that was cold, narrow, concentrated and powerful. Webster considered him "much the ablest man in the Senate," the greatest in fact that he had met in his entire public life. "He could have," he declared, "demolished Newton, Calvin or even John Locke as a logician."

His speeches, stripped of all excess verbiage, marched across the Senate floor in even columns, measured, disciplined, carrying all before them. Strangely enough, although he had the appearance, especially in his later days, of a fanatic, he was a man of infinite charm and personality. He was reputed to be the best conversationalist in South Carolina, and he won to him through their emotions men who failed to comprehend his closely reasoned arguments. His hold upon the imagination and affection of the entire South steadily grew, and at his death in the midst of the great debate of 1850 he was universally mourned.

Calhoun believed that the Constitutional Convention had not nationalized our government; that the sovereign states still retained "the right of judging . . . when the Congress encroached upon the individual state's power and liberty."

With other Southerners, he believed that the geography and climate of the western country made it unlikely that slavery could ever prosper in many of the territories that were seeking to become states, and that only in the Southwest could they hope to balance the surging tide of free western states by securing new slave states and Senators from the lands seized from Mexico. The Clay Compromise of 1850, which sought to conciliate the differences between North and South as to the ultimate fate of these lands, thus assumed far-reaching importance.

All of the currents of conflict and disunion, of growth and decline, of strength and weakness, came to a climax in 1850.

The three chief protagonists in the Washington drama of 1850 had been colleagues in Congress as far back as 1813. Then they were young, full of pride and passion and hope, and the world lay waiting before them. Now nearly forty years later in the sunset of their lives—for they would all be dead within two years—with youth and illusions gone, they moved once again to the center of the stage.

But they were not alone in the struggle. Neither Senator Thomas Hart Benton nor Sam Houston was dwarfed by the towering reputations of his three colleagues. Each was a legend in his own lifetime—and occupying respectively the strategic border states of Missouri and Texas, it was inevitable that the choice that each would make as the country slowly drifted apart would affect the nature and outcome of the general struggle.

That secession did not occur in 1850 instead of 1861 is due in great part to Daniel Webster, who was in large measure responsible for the country's acceptance of Henry Clay's compromise. The reasons he supported the compromise, the effect of his support and the calumnies he suffered are detailed in Chapter 2.

That the key border state of Missouri did not join the Confederacy in 1861 was due in good measure to the memory of its former Senator Thomas Hart Benton. No man gave more than Senator Benton for the preservation of the Union. His efforts and his fate are told in Chapter 3.

Texas joined the Confederacy, but not without a struggle that made Senator Houston's old age a shipwreck. His story is told in Chapter 4.

DANIEL WEBSTER

". . . not as a Massachusetts man
but as an American . . ."

THE BLIZZARDY NIGHT of January 21, 1850, was no
night in Washington for an ailing old man to be
out. But wheezing and coughing fitfully, Henry
Clay made his way through the snowdrifts to the
home of Daniel Webster. He had a plan—a plan
to save the Union—and he knew he must have the
support of the North's most renowned orator and
statesman. He knew that he had no time to lose,
for that very afternoon President Taylor, in a
message to Congress asking California's admission
as a free state, had only thrown fuel on the raging
fire that threatened to consume the Union. Why
had the President failed to mention New Mexico,
asked the North? What about the Fugitive Slave
Law being enforced, said the South? What about
the District of Columbia slave trade, Utah, Texas
boundaries? Tempers mounted, plots unfolded,
disunity was abroad in the land.

But Henry Clay had a plan—a plan for another

Clay battles a blizzard to reach Webster's home.

Great Compromise to preserve the nation. For an hour he outlined its contents to Daniel Webster in the warmth of the latter's comfortable home, and together they talked of saving the Union. Few meetings in American history have ever been so productive or so ironic in their consequences. For the Compromise of 1850 added to Henry Clay's garlands as the great Pacificator; but Daniel Webster's support which insured its success resulted in his political crucifixion, and, for half a century or more, his historical condemnation.

The man upon whom Henry Clay called that

wintry night was one of the most extraordinary figures in American political history. Daniel Webster is familiar to many of us today as the battler for Jabez Stone's soul against the devil in Stephen Vincent Benét's story. But in his own lifetime, he had many battles against the devil for his own soul—and some he lost. Webster, wrote one of his intimate friends, was "a compound of strength and weakness, dust and divinity," or in Emerson's words "a great man with a small ambition."

There could be no mistaking he was a great man —he looked like one, talked like one, was treated like one and insisted he was one. With all his faults and failings, Daniel Webster was undoubtedly the most talented figure in our Congressional history: not in his ability to win men to a cause—he was no match in that with Henry Clay; not in his ability to hammer out a philosophy of government—Calhoun outshone him there; but in his ability to make alive and supreme the latent sense of oneness, of Union, that all Americans felt but which few could express.

A very slow speaker, hardly averaging a hundred words a minute, Webster combined the musical charm of his deep organ-like voice, a vivid imagination, an ability to crush his opponents with a barrage of facts, a confident and deliberate manner of speaking and a striking appearance to make his orations a magnet that drew crowds hurrying to the Senate chamber. He prepared his speeches with the utmost care, but seldom wrote them out in a prepared text. It has been said that he could think out a speech sentence by sentence, correct the sentences in his mind without the use of a pencil and then deliver it exactly as he thought it out.

Certainly that striking appearance was half the secret of his power, and convinced all who looked upon his face that he was one born to rule men. Although less than six feet tall, Webster's slender frame when contrasted with the magnificent sweep of his shoulders gave him a theatrical but formidable presence. But it was his extraordinary head that contemporaries found so memorable, with the features Carlyle described for all to remember: "The tanned complexion, the amorphous crag-like face; the dull black eyes under the precipice of brows, like dull anthracite furnaces needing only to be blown; the mastiff mouth accurately closed." One contemporary called Webster "a living lie, because no man on earth could be so great as he looked."

But whatever his faults, Daniel Webster remained the greatest orator of his day, the leading

member of the American Bar, one of the most re-
nowned leaders of the Whig party, and the only
Senator capable of checking Calhoun. And thus
Henry Clay knew he must enlist these extraor-
dinary talents on behalf of his Great Compromise.
Time and events proved he was right.

As the God-like Daniel listened in thoughtful
silence, the sickly Clay unfolded his last great
effort to hold the Union together. Its key features
were five in number: (1) California was to be
admitted as a free (nonslaveholding) state; (2)
New Mexico and Utah were to be organized as
territories without legislation either for or against
slavery, thus running directly contrary to the hotly
debated Wilmot Proviso which was intended to
prohibit slavery in the new territories; (3) Texas
was to be compensated for some territory to be
ceded to New Mexico; (4) the slave trade would
be abolished in the District of Columbia; and (5)
a more stringent and enforceable Fugitive Slave
Law was to be enacted to guarantee return to
their masters of runaway slaves captured in Northern states. The Compromise would be condemned
by the Southern extremists as appeasement, chiefly
on its first and fourth provisions; and by the Northern abolitionists as 90 per cent concessions to the
South with a meaningless 10 per cent sop thrown

to the North, particularly because of the second and fifth provisions. Few Northerners could stomach any strengthening of the Fugitive Slave Act, the most bitterly hated measure—and until prohibition, the most flagrantly disobeyed—ever passed by Congress. Massachusetts had even enacted a law making it a crime for anyone to enforce the provisions of the Act in that state!

How could Henry Clay then hope to win to such a plan Daniel Webster of Massachusetts? Was he not specifically on record as a consistent foe of slavery and a supporter of the Wilmot Proviso? Had he not told the Senate in the Oregon Debate:

> I shall oppose all slavery extension and all increase of slave representation in all places, at all times, under all circumstances, even against all inducements, against all supposed limitation of great interests, against all combinations, against all compromises.

That very week he had written a friend: "From my earliest youth, I have regarded slavery as a great moral and political evil. . . . You need not fear that I shall vote for any compromise or do anything inconsistent with the past."

But Daniel Webster feared that civil violence "would only rivet the chains of slavery the more strongly." And the preservation of the Union was far dearer to his heart than his opposition to slavery.

And thus on that fateful January night, Daniel Webster promised Henry Clay his conditional support, and took inventory of the crisis about him. At first he shared the views of those critics and historians who scoffed at the possibility of secession in 1850. But as he talked with Southern leaders and observed "the condition of the country, I thought the inevitable consequences of leaving the existing controversies unadjusted would be Civil War." "I am nearly broken down with labor and anxiety," he wrote his son, "I know not how to meet the present emergency, or with what weapons to beat down the Northern and Southern follies now raging in equal extremes. . . . I have poor spirits and little courage."

Two groups were threatening in 1850 to break away from the United States of America. In New England, Garrison was publicly proclaiming, "I am an Abolitionist and, therefore, for the dissolution of the Union." And a mass meeting of Northern Abolitionists declared that "the Constitution is a covenant with death and an agreement with hell." In the South, Calhoun was writing a friend in February of 1850, "Disunion is the only alternative that is left for us." And in his last great ad-

dress to the Senate, read for him on March 4, only
a few short weeks before his death, while he sa
by too feeble to speak, he declared, "The South
will be forced to choose between abolition and se
cession."

A preliminary convention of Southerners, also
instigated by Calhoun, urged a full-scale conven
tion of the South at Nashville for June of that fate
ful year to popularize the idea of dissolution.

The time was ripe for secession, and few were
prepared to speak for Union. Even Alexander
Stephens of Georgia, anxious to preserve the
Union, wrote friends in the South who were sympathetic with his views that "the feeling among
the Southern members for a dissolution of the
Union . . . is becoming much more general. Mer
are now beginning to talk of it seriously who
twelve months ago hardly permitted themselves
to think of it. . . . the crisis is not far ahead. . .
A dismemberment of this Republic I now consider
inevitable." During the critical month preceding
Webster's speech, six Southern states, each to secede ten years later, approved the aims of the
Nashville Convention and appointed delegates.

Such was the perilous state of the nation in the
early months of 1850.

By the end of February, the Senator from Massachusetts had determined upon his course. Only the Clay Compromise, Daniel Webster decided, could avert secession and civil war; and he wrote a friend that he planned "to make an honest truth-telling speech and a Union speech, and discharge a clear conscience." As he set to work preparing his notes, he received abundant warning of the attacks his message would provoke. His constituents and Massachusetts newspapers admonished him strongly not to waver in his consistent anti-slavery stand, and many urged him to employ still tougher tones against the South. But the Senator from Massachusetts had made up his mind, as he told his friends on March 6, "to push my skiff from the shore alone." He would act according to the creed with which he had challenged the Senate several years earlier:

Inconsistencies of opinion arising from changes of circumstances are often justifiable. But there is one sort of inconsistency that is culpable: it is the inconsistency between a man's conviction and his vote, between his conscience and his conduct. No man shall ever charge me with an inconsistency of that kind.

And so came the 7th of March, 1850.

Realizing after months of insomnia that this might be the last great effort his health would permit, Webster stimulated his strength for the speech by oxide of arsenic and other drugs, and devoted the morning to polishing up his notes. Two hours before the Senate was to meet—the chamber, the galleries, the anterooms and even the corridors of the Capitol were filled with those who had been traveling for days from all parts of the nation to hear Daniel Webster.

Then as he rose slowly to his feet, the crowd fell silent. All eyes were fixed on the speaker; no spectator save his own son knew what he would say.

Summoning for the last time that spellbinding oratorical ability, he abandoned his previous opposition to slavery in the territories, abandoned his constituents' abhorrence of the Fugitive Slave Law, abandoned his own place in the history and hearts of his countrymen and abandoned his last chance for the goal that had eluded him for over twenty years—the Presidency. Daniel Webster preferred to risk his career and his reputation rather than risk the Union.

"Mr. President," he began, "I wish to speak today, not as a Massachusetts man, nor as a Northern man, but as an American and a Member of the Senate of the United States. . . . I speak today for the preservation of the Union. Hear me for my cause."

Daniel Webster pleads the Union cause.

For three hours and eleven minutes, with only a few references to his extensive notes, Daniel Webster pleaded the Union's cause. Relating the grievances of each side, he asked for conciliation and understanding in the name of patriotism. The Senate's main concern, he insisted, was neither to promote slavery nor to abolish it, but to preserve the United States of America. And with telling logic and remarkable foresight he bitterly attacked the idea of "peaceable secession":

Sir, your eyes and mine are never destined to see that miracle. The dismemberment of this vast country without convulsion! Who is so foolish . . . as to expect to see any such thing? . . . Instead of speaking of the possibility or utility of secession, instead of dwelling in those caverns of darkness, . . . let us enjoy the fresh air of liberty and union. . . . Let us make our generation one of the strongest and brightest links in that golden chain which is destined, I fondly believe, to grapple the people of all the states to this Constitution for ages to come.

And so the danger of immediate secession and bloodshed passed. As Senator Winthrop remarked, Webster's speech had "disarmed and quieted the South [and] knocked the Nashville Convention into a cocked hat." The *Journal of Commerce* was to remark in later months that "Webster did more than any other man in the whole country, and at a greater hazard of personal popularity, to stem and roll back the torrent of sectionalism which in 1850 threatened to overthrow the pillars of the Constitution and the Union."

The spirit of conciliation in Webster's speech gave the North the righteous feeling that it had made every attempt to treat the South with fairness, and the defenders of the Union were thus united more strongly against what they felt to be Southern violations of those compromises ten years later. Even from the military point of view of the North, postponement of the battle for ten years enabled the Northern states to increase tremendously their lead in popularity, voting power, production and railroads.

Undoubtedly this was understood by many of Webster's supporters, including the business and professional men of Massachusetts who helped distribute hundreds of thousands of copies of the Seventh of March speech throughout the country.

But it was not understood by the Abolitionists and Free Soilers of 1850. A mass meeting in Faneuil Hall condemned the speech as "unworthy of a wise statesman and a good man," and resolved that "Constitution or no Constitution, law or no law, we will not allow a fugitive slave to be taken from the state of Massachusetts." As the Massachusetts Legislature enacted further resolutions wholly contrary to the spirit of the Seventh of March speech, one member called Webster "a recreant son of Massachusetts who misrepresents her in the Senate"; and another stated that "Daniel Webster will be a fortunate man if God, in his sparing mercy, shall preserve his life long enough for him to repent of this act and efface this stain on his name."

Daniel Webster was humiliated for all time in

the literature of our land by the cutting words of
the usually gentle John Greenleaf Whittier in his
immortal poem "Ichabod":

> So fallen! so lost! the light withdrawn
>> Which once he wore!
> The glory from his gray hairs gone
>> Forevermore! . . .
>
> Of all we loved and honored, naught
>> Save power remains;
> A fallen angel's pride of thought,
>> Still strong in chains. . . .
>
> Then pay the reverence of old days
>> To his dead fame;
> Walk backward, with averted gaze,
>> And hide the shame!

Years afterward Whittier was to recall that he
penned this acid verse "in one of the saddest
moments of my life." And for Daniel Webster, the
arrogant, scornful giant of the ages who believed
himself above political rancor, Whittier's attack
was especially bitter. To some extent he had attempted to shrug off his attackers, stating that he
had expected to be libeled and abused, particularly by the Abolitionists and intellectuals who had
previously scorned him, much as George Washington and others before him had been abused. To

those who urged a prompt reply, he merely related the story of the old deacon in a similar predicament who told his friends, "I always make it a rule never to clean up the path until the snow is done falling."

The following year, despite his seventy years, Webster went on extended speaking tours defending his position: "If the chances had been one in a thousand that Civil War would be the result, I should still have felt that thousandth chance should be guarded against by any reasonable sacrifice." When his efforts—and those of Clay, Douglas and others—on behalf of compromise were ultimately successful, he noted sarcastically that many of his colleagues were now saying "They always meant to stand by the Union to the last."

But Daniel Webster was doomed to disappointment in his hopes that this latent support might again enable him to seek the Presidency. For his speech had so thoroughly destroyed those prospects that the recurring popularity of his position could not possibly satisfy the great masses of voters in New England and the North. He could not receive the Presidential nomination he had so long desired; but neither could he ever put to rest the assertion, which was not only expressed by his contemporary critics but subsequently by several nineteenth-century historians, that his real objective in the Seventh of March speech was a bid for Southern support for the Presidency.

But this "profound selfishness," which Emerson was so certain the speech represented, could not have entered into Daniel Webster's motivations. "Had he been bidding for the Presidency," as Professor Nevins points out, "he would have trimmed his phrases and inserted weasel-words upon New Mexico and the fugitive slaves. The first precaution of any aspirant for the Presidency is to make sure of his own state and section; and Webster knew that his speech would send echoes of denunciation leaping from Mount Mansfield to Monamoy Light."

So Daniel Webster, who neither could have intended his speech as an improvement of his political popularity nor permitted his ambitions to weaken his plea for the Union, died a disappointed and discouraged death in 1852, his eyes fixed on the flag flying from the mast of the sailboat he had anchored in view of his bedroom window. But to the very end he was true to character, asking on his deathbed, "Wife, children, doctor, I trust on this occasion I have said nothing unworthy of Daniel Webster." And to the end he had been true to the Union, and to his greatest act of courageous principle; for in his last words to the Senate, Webster had written his own epitaph:

I shall stand by the Union . . . with absolute disregard of personal consequences. What are personal consequences . . . in comparison with the good or evil which may befall a great country in a crisis like this? . . . Let the consequences be what they will, I am careless. No man can suffer too much, and no man can fall too soon, if he suffer or if he fall in defense of the liberties and Constitution of his country.

THOMAS HART BENTON

"I despise the bubble popularity . . ."

"MR. PRESIDENT, SIR . . ." A burly, black-haired Senator was speaking to a nearly empty chamber in 1850. Those who remained, including a nervous Senator who had just termed the speaker quarrelsome, saw his great muscles tighten and his sweeping shoulders become icily erect, and heard his hard, cold voice rasp out the word "sir" like a poisoned dart from his massive, Romanesque head.

"Mr. President, sir . . . I never quarrel, sir. But sometimes I fight, sir; and whenever I fight, sir, a funeral follows, sir."

No one regarded this as an idle boast by the senior Senator from Missouri, Thomas Hart Benton. True, he had not killed a man since his early days in St. Louis, when a U.S. District Attorney had the misfortune to engage the rugged Missourian in a duel (at nine feet!). But all the Senate knew that Thomas Hart Benton was a rough and tumble fighter off and on the Senate floor—no longer with pistols but with stinging sarcasm, vituperative though learned oratory and bitterly heated debate. He himself was immune to the wounds of those political clashes from which his adversaries retired bleeding and broken. For his great ego and vigorous health had made him thick-skinned mentally as well as physically. (The leathery quality of his skin was in part the result of a daily brushing with a horsehair brush "because, sir, the Roman gladiators did it, sir." When asked if the brush was truly rough, he would roar: "Why, sir, if I were to touch you with that brush, sir, you would cry murder, sir!")

Benton had championed the West with a boundless energy. The Pony Express, the telegraph line and the highways to the interior were among his proud accomplishments—and a transcontinental railroad and fully developed West, rich in population and resources, were among his dreams. Defeat Benton, father of the Senate and defender of the people? "Nobody opposes Benton, sir," he would roar.

But by 1844, the handwriting of inevitable defeat had already appeared on the wall. Missouri, a slave state, gradually came to feel more strongly that her allegiance belonged to her sister states of the South. She tended to look with increasing suspicion upon her rebellious Senator whose primary loyalty was neither to his party nor his section, but to the Union.

As the campaign for the legislature which would consider his re-election began in 1844, Benton broke sharply with his state and party by engineering the defeat of the treaty for the annexation of Texas.

His tremendous personal popularity among the ordinary citizens carried him through the legislature—but by only eight votes, in a legislature his party controlled by a twenty-seven vote margin. Senator Benton could hardly mistake the ominous unwritten instructions of his state—in effect: "temper your independent tongue."

Despite his near defeat in 1844-45, Senator Benton audaciously opposed his party and state on the Oregon expansion issue. Having personally aroused intense public approval for expansion—particularly in Missouri, which had sent large numbers of its citizens to Oregon—he now felt that the Democratic "whole of Oregon or none," "fifty-four forty or fight" position was extravagantly unrealistic. Counseling President Polk against adhering to those slogans in dealing with England and Canada, he assailed his Democratic colleagues in the Senate for their refusal to concede the error of their views —especially Michigan's Lewis Cass. Explaining that the "simples" was a kind of disease which made Missouri horses physically and mentally blind, and which could be cured only when the veterinary cut a certain nerve, he announced that he had "cut Cass for the simples, sir, and cured him."

Again he was assailed as a coward and traitor. His biographer believes that "probably no man in history has been more vilified than he was at this time."

The beginning of Benton's end—so strongly suggested already by the antagonisms he had aroused over Texas and Oregon—came on February 19, 1847. John C. Calhoun read to a worried Senate his famous resolutions insisting that Congress had no right to interfere with the development of slavery in the territories. Later events indicated the correctness of Benton's views that those resolutions were but "firebrands intended for electioneering and disunion purposes," providing the slave states with a program on which to unite—not only as a section but behind the leadership and Presidential candidacy of Calhoun himself. Nevertheless, Calhoun called for an immediate vote; and in the momentary confusion that followed, he was angrily amazed to see the massive and stately Benton rising from his chair, his face flashing with

obvious contempt for Calhoun, the resolutions and
his own political fate.

> Mr. Benton: Mr. President, we have some business
> to transact, and I do not intend to avoid business for
> a string of abstractions.
>
> Mr. Calhoun: . . . I certainly supposed the Senator
> from Missouri, the representative of a slaveholding
> state, would have supported these resolutions . . .
>
> Mr. Benton: The Senator knows very well from my
> whole course in public life that I would never leave
> public business to take up firebrands to set the world
> on fire.
>
> Mr. Calhoun: Then I shall know where to find the
> gentleman.
>
> Mr. Benton: I shall be found in the right place . . .
> on the side of my country and the Union. ["This
> answer," wrote Benton in later years, "given on that
> day and on that spot, is one of the incidents of his
> life which Mr. Benton will wish posterity to remem-
> ber."]

Finally, when in 1848 the slavery issue split the
Democratic party at its convention, Benton, de-
ploring the split and denying the importance of
the issue, refused to support either camp actively.
He was now a man without a party, a politician
without a recognized platform, and a Senator without a constituency.

In 1849 Calhoun denounced Benton to his Mis-

souri enemies as one "false to the South for the
last ten years. . . . He can do us much less injury
in the camp of the abolitionists than he could in
our own camp. His will be the fate of all traitors."
By an overwhelming margin, the Missouri Legislature expressed Missouri's desire to cooperate with
other slaveholding states, and instructed her Senators to vote accordingly.

Determined to see the Legislature repudiated,
Benton launched an aggressive tour of his hostile
state.

One day, bitterly reading and commenting upon
the names of each member of the legislature, he
stopped when he came to the "D's" and said he
smelled a Nullifier. A legislator named Davies having arisen to protest, Benton scowled: "I never
called your name, sir. Turn your profile to the audience. . . . [Like a fool, Davies complied] . . . Citizens, that is not the profile of a man; it is the profile
of a dog." When an old friend, accidentally failing
to remove his hat, asked a question in the middle of
a speech, Benton angrily scolded, "Who is this
man, citizens, who dares to stop Benton in his
speech?" "Aycock, Colonel Aycock," came a dozen
voices. "Aycock? No, citizens, no; not a cock; but
a hen rather. Take off your hat, sir, and take your
seat."

When he mounted the platform at Fayette, where his life had been threatened if he dared enter the city limits, a body of armed men began an uproar. But according to the Jefferson *Inquirer* "in a quarter of an hour the insulters were cowed; and the speech for four hours was received with respect and applause."

But Benton's turbulent tour could not stem a tide much greater than any one man or single state. A friend of Benton's wrote:

> I am sorry Mr. Benton indulges in so much profanity. Yet in this respect his opponents . . . are not a whit behind. Nine out of twenty-two Democratic papers in the state are unbounded in vilifying him with such epithets as traitor, apostate, scoundrel, barn burner, abolitionist and free-soiler . . . I am afraid Benton will be defeated.

Even his gigantic ego could not have hidden from Thomas Hart Benton the unmistakable fact that this was his last term—unless. Would he initiate a convention of all Missouri Democrats to settle his differences with the proslavery camp? "I would sooner," he thundered, "sit in council with the six thousand dead who have died of cholera in St. Louis than go into convention with such a gang of scamps!" Would he speak one word for the South in the great debate of 1850 on the

Clay Compromise, or at least remain silent in order to save the seat he loved for future battles? He would not. As a Missouri associate recalled: "... At an early period of his existence, while reading Plutarch, he determined that if it should ever become necessary for the good of his country, he would sacrifice his own political existence."

As the contest for the State Legislature that would name his successor raged in Missouri, Senator Benton stood fast by his post in Washington, outspoken to the end in his condemnation of the views his constituents now embraced. Willing to meet crushing defeat rather than compromise his principles (for as Clay said, intending it to be disparaging, Benton had the "hide of a hippopotamus"), he towered over his more famous colleagues in terms of sheer moral courage. Now isolated from his political friends in the West and South, and yet maintaining his distaste for the abolitionists, whom he held equally responsible for splitting the Union, Benton steered an extraordinarily independent course in his vituperative attacks on Clay's compromise.

During the course of the year, still another melodramatic event—termed "the greatest indignity the Senate had ever suffered"—served to show the bitter feelings of the South toward

Benton. The peppery Senator Henry Foote of
Mississippi, no blind follower of Calhoun but suspected by Benton of helping plot his defeat in
Missouri, took the floor on several occasions to
abuse Benton's position in a coarse manner ex-
ceeding even the Missourian's own rhetorical ex-
cesses. Taunting him with his approaching defeat
in Missouri, and stinging under Benton's counter-
attack, Foote ridiculed Benton as one "shielded by
his age . . . and shielded by his own established
cowardice."

Finally Benton announced that, if the Senate
failed to protect him from such "false and cow-
ardly" attacks, he intended "to protect himself,
cost what it may." On April 17, in the midst of another verbal assault upon him by Foote, Benton
advanced toward the Mississippian, then turned
back at a colleague's restraining touch. Suddenly
Foote whipped out a pistol and pointed it at Benton, who dramatically threw open his coat and
cried: "I have no pistol! Let him fire! Let the
assassin fire!"

No one fired. The Senate was shocked—although its special committee on censure barely
rapped the knuckles of the two participants—but
verbal assaults between the two did not cease.
When Benton heard of Foote's threat that he in-

*"I have no pistol! Let him fire!
Let the assassin fire!"*

tended to write a small book in which *l'affaire*
Benton would play a leading role, Benton replied:
"Tell Foote that I shall write a very large book in
which he will not figure at all!" (And he did.)

In January, 1851, climaxing a bitter twelve-day
struggle, the Missouri Legislature on its fortieth
ballot elected a Whig. After thirty years of out
standing statesmanship in the Senate of the
United States, Thomas Hart Benton was ignomini
ously dismissed from the service and called home

Undismayed, and still stubbornly refusing to
follow the easy path to a graceful and popular
political retirement, Benton fought to return to
Congress the following year as Representative
from St. Louis. His campaign, according to the
opposition New Orleans *Crescent*, "spared no
public or personal denunciation. He exhausted
every expletive of abuse. He ransacked the entire
range of the English language for terms of scorn
and derision." Elected in one final burst of persona
popularity, he promptly threw to the winds all
chances for future re-election by delivering one of
his most memorable, and one of his most vitupera
tive, speeches in opposition to the chief measure
of his party, the Kansas-Nebraska Bill.

Soundly defeated for re-election in 1854, and
grieved by the death of his beloved wife, Benton

was not yet ready to submit. In vain he sought re-election to the Senate in 1855; and, at the age of seventy-four, made one last, hopeless race for Governor in 1856. Jessie Benton Frémont revealed in her memoirs that her courageous father, suffering from what he knew to be a fatal throat cancer, could speak in public only by maintaining absolute silence for several days in advance. Even then his throat bled during and following his still ferocious speeches. Yet he traveled more than twelve hundred miles in a desperate speaking tour to defeat the Whig and anti-Benton Democratic candidates, and he returned home, defeated but proud, to complete his monumental historical works.

He died while still hard at work, using an amanuensis when his feeble hands could no longer grasp a pen, and uncomplaining even to his last whispered words: "I am comfortable, I am content." His death, mourned throughout the nation, revealed how little wealth his upright career had accumulated for his daughters.

But even in death and defeat, Thomas Hart Benton was victorious. For his voice from the past on behalf of Union was one of the deciding factors that prevented Missouri from yielding to all the desperate efforts to drive her into secession along with her sister slave states. Fate had borne out the wisdom of Benton's last report to his constituents as Senator: "I value solid popularity—the esteem of good men for good action. I despise the bubble popularity that is won without merit and lost without crime. . . . I have been Senator 30 years. . . . I sometimes had to act against the preconceived opinions and first impressions of my constituents; but always with full reliance upon their intelligence to understand me and their equity to do me justice—*and I have never been disappointed.*"

SAM HOUSTON

". . . I can forget that I am called a traitor."

THE FIRST RAYS OF DAWN were streaking into the ill-lit Senate chamber of 1854 as one final speaker rose to seek recognition. Weary, haggard and unshaven Senators, slumped despondently in their chairs after the rigors of an all-night session, muttered "Vote, Vote" in the hopes of discouraging any further oratory on a bill already certain of passage. But Senator Sam Houston of Texas, the hero of San Jacinto, was not easily discouraged by overwhelming odds; and as his deep, musical voice carried the bold if unpolished words of a powerful message to his astonished colleagues, they shook off the dull stupor which had deadened their fatigued brains and sat upright and attentive.

The bill on which bitter and exhausting debate now closed was known as the Kansas-Nebraska Bill, the new "unity" device of the Democratic party and the latest concession to the South. It repealed the Missouri Compromise of 1820, and reopened the slavery extension issue thought settled in the Compromise of 1850, by permitting the residents of that vast territory from Iowa to the Rockies to decide the slavery question for themselves, on the assumption that the northern part of the territory would be free and the southern part slave. For Democrats and Southerners, this bill had become "must" legislation.

Sam Houston was a Democrat of long standing. And Sam Houston was a Southerner by birth, residence, loyalty and philosophy. But Sam Houston was also Sam Houston, one of the most independent, unique, popular, forceful and dramatic individuals ever to enter the Senate chamber. The first Senator from Texas, his name had long before been a household word as Commander in Chief of those straggling and undermanned Texas volunteers who routed the entire Mexican Army at San Jacinto, captured its general and established the independence of Texas. He had been acclaimed as the first President of the Independent Republic of Texas, a Member of her Congress, and President again before the admission of Texas into the Union as a state. He was no easy mark at the age of sixty-four, and neither sectional nor party ties were enough to seal his lips.

Houston must have known the bill would pass, he must have known that not a single other Southern Democrat would join him. But, standing erect, his chin thrust forward, picturesque if not eccentric in his military cloak and panther-skin waistcoat (at times he appeared in a vast sombrero and Mexican blanket), Sam Houston, the "magnificent barbarian," made one of his rare speeches to a weary but attentive Senate:

This is an eminently perilous measure; and do you expect me to remain here silent, or to shrink from the discharge of my duty in admonishing the South of what I conceive the results will be? I will speak in spite of all the intimidations, or threats, or discountenances that may be thrown upon me. Sir, the charge that I am going with the Abolitionists or Free-Soilers affects me not. The discharge of conscious duty prompts me often to confront the united array of the very section of the country in which I reside, in which my associations are, in which my affections rest. . . . Sir, if this is a boon that is offered to propitiate the South, I, as a Southern man, repudiate it. I will have none of it. . . . Our children are either to live in after times in the enjoyment of peace, of harmony, and prosperity, or the alternative remains for them of anarchy, discord, and civil broil. We can avert the last. I trust we shall. . . . I adjure you to regard the contract once made to harmonize and preserve this Union. Maintain the Missouri Compromise! Stir not up agitation! Give us peace!

His lonely vote against the Kansas-Nebraska Bill, on that stormy dawn in 1854, was indeed the "last straw." It was loudly whispered about the Senate that this was the last term for the colorful General.

The contradictions in the life of Sam Houston a century ago may seem irreconcilable today. Houston himself remains a mystery to the careful historian of today.

He was fiercely ambitious, yet at the end he sacrificed for principle all he had ever won or wanted. He was a Southerner, and yet he steadfastly maintained his loyalty to the Union. He was a slaveholder who defended the right of Northern ministers to petition Congress against slavery; he was a notorious drinker who took the vow of temperance; he was an adopted son of the Cherokee Indians who won his first military honors fighting the Creeks; he was a Governor of Tennessee but a Senator from Texas. He was in turn magnanimous yet vindictive, affectionate yet cruel, eccentric yet self-conscious, faithful yet opportunistic. But Sam Houston's contradictions actually confirm his one basic, consistent quality: indomitable individualism, sometimes spectacular, sometimes

crude, sometimes mysterious, but always courageous.

In the 1857 election Houston announced himself a candidate for Governor of Texas. He would
not run as a Democrat, or as the candidate of any
faction or newspaper—or even resign from the Senate. He would run as Sam Houston, to "regenerate
the politics of the state. The people want excitement and I had as well give it as anyone."

And plenty of excitement is what he provided.
He harangued audiences in every corner of Texas
with his great fund of vituperative epithets and
withering sarcasm. When refused the right to
speak in the county courthouse at one stop on his
campaign tour, he assured the crowd it was quite
all right,

> I am not a taxpayer here. I did not contribute to
> buy a single brick or nail in this building and have
> no right to speak here. But if there is a man within
> the sound of my voice who would desire to hear
> Sam Houston speak and will follow me to yonder
> hillside, I have a right to speak on the soil of Texas
> because I have watered it with my blood.

But his votes on Kansas and other Southern
measures could not be explained away to an angry
constituency, and Texas handed Sam Houston the
first trouncing of his political career. He ought to

resign from the Senate now, said the antagonistic *Gazette*, instead of "holding on to the barren office . . . merely to receive his per diem allowance." But Sam Houston, encouraged that the margin of his defeat was no greater than three to two, returned to Washington for his final years in the Senate unshaken in his beliefs. On November 10, 1857, Sam Houston was unceremoniously dismissed by the Texas Legislature and a more militant spokesman for the South elected as his successor.

We cannot conclude our story of Senator Sam Houston's political courage with his retirement from the Senate. Returning to his ranch in Texas, the doughty ex-Senator found he was unable to retire when the Governor who had defeated him two years previously was threatening to lead the state into secession. So in the fall of 1859, the aging warrior again ran as an independent candidate for Governor, again with no party, no newspaper and no organization behind him, and making but one campaign speech. He would rely, he told his audience in that still fascinating voice, "upon the Constitution and the Union, all the old Jacksonian democracy I ever professed or officially practiced. . . . In politics I am an old fogy because I cling devotedly to those primitive principles upon which our government was founded.

It was a bitter campaign, the Democrats and
newspapers assailing Houston with acrimonious
passion, reopening old charges of Houston's im-
morality and cowardice. But strangely enough,
the appeal of the issues (however premature) he
had raised, his personal following among his old
comrades, disgust with the administration of his
opponents, new popularity which Houston had acquired just prior to his retirement by his exposure
on the Senate floor of a corrupt federal judge, and
a surge of sentimental feeling toward him upon his
return to his beloved Texas, all combined to elect
Sam Houston Governor in a complete reversal of
his defeat two years earlier.

As sentiment grew overwhelmingly in favor of
secession during the heated Presidential campaign of 1860, Governor Houston could only im-
plore his impatient constituents to wait and see
what Mr. Lincoln's attitude would be, if elected.
But the fact that he had received a few unsolicited
votes in the Republican Convention as Lincoln's
running mate furnished further ammunition to
his enemies. And when the town of Henderson
mysteriously burned in August, the Governor
could do nothing to prevent the wave of lynch-
ings, vigilante committees and angry sentiment
which followed rumors of Negro uprisings and

arson. Houston's speech in Waco denouncing secession was answered by the explosion of a keg of powder behind the hotel in which he slept unharmed. But heedless of personal or political danger, he arose from a sickbed in September to make one final appeal:

> I ask not the defeat of sectionalism by sectionalism, but by nationality. . . . These are no new sentiments to me. I uttered them in the American Senate in 1856. I utter them now. I was denounced then as a traitor. I am denounced now. Be it so! Men who never endured the privation, the toil, the peril that I have for my country call me a traitor because I am willing to yield obedience to the Constitution and the constituted authorities. Let them suffer what I have for this Union, and they will feel it entwining so closely around their hearts that it will be like snapping the cords of life to give it up. . . . What are the people who call me a traitor? Are they those who march under the national flag and are ready to defend it? That is my banner! . . . and so long as it waves proudly o'er me, even as it has waved amid stormy scenes where these men were not, I can forget that I am called a traitor.

Abraham Lincoln was elected President, and immediately throughout Texas the Lone Star flag was hoisted in an atmosphere of excited and belligerent expectation. Houston's plea that Texas fight for her rights "in the Union and for the sake of the Union" fell on deaf ears. "A sentiment of servility" snapped the press; and Governor Houston was shoved aside as a Secession Convention was called.

On the day the Ordinance of Secession was to be adopted, Sam Houston sat on the platform, grimly silent, his presence renewing the courage of those few friends of Union who remained in the hall. "To those who tell of his wonderful charge up the hill at San Jacinto," said the historian Wharton, "I say it took a thousand times more courage when he stalked into the Secession Convention at Austin and alone defied and awed them." When, encouraged by the magic of Houston's presence, James W. Throckmorton cast one of the seven votes against secession, he was loudly and bitterly hissed; and rising in his place he made the memorable reply, "When the rabble hiss, well may patriots tremble."

But there were few who trembled as the Ordinance was adopted and submitted to the people for their approval at the polls one month later. Immediately the fighting ex-Senator took the stump in a one-man campaign to keep Texas in the Union. Ugly crowds, stones and denunciation as a traitor met him throughout the state. At Waco

Sam Houston looks the armed thug in the eye.

his life was threatened. At Belton, an armed thug
suddenly arose and started toward him. But old
Sam Houston, looking him right in the eye, put
each hand on his own pistols: "Ladies and Gentle-
men, keep your seats. It is nothing but a fice bark-
ing at the lion in his den." Unharmed, he stalked
the state in characteristic fashion, confounding his
enemies with powerful sarcasm. Asked to express
his honest opinion of the secessionist leader, Houston replied: "He has all the characteristics of a dog
except fidelity." Now seventy years old, but still
an impressively straight figure with those pene-
trating eyes and massive white hair, Old Sam
closed his tour in Galveston before a jeering and
ugly mob. "Some of you laugh to scorn the idea
of bloodshed as the result of secession," he cried,
"but let me tell you what is coming. You may,
after the sacrifice of countless millions of treasures
and hundreds of thousands of precious lives, as a
bare possibility, win Southern independence, if
God be not against you. But I doubt it. The North
is determined to preserve this Union."

His prophecy was unheeded. On February 23,
Texas voted for secession by a large margin; and
on March 2, the anniversary of Houston's birthday
and Texan independence, the special convention
reassembled at Austin and declared that Texas

had seceded. Governor Houston, still desperately attempting to regain the initiative, indicated he would make known his plans on the matter to the legislature. Angry at his insistence that its legal authority had ended, the Convention by a thumping vote of 109-2 declared Texas to be a part of the Southern Confederacy, and decreed that all state officers must take the new oath of allegiance on the fourteenth of March. The Governor's secretary merely replied that Governor Houston "did not acknowledge the existence of the Convention and should not regard its action as binding upon him."

On March 14, as an eyewitness described it, the Convention hall was "crowded . . . electrified with fiery radiations, of men tingling with passion, and glowing and burning with the anticipation of revengeful battle. The air was full of the stirring clamor of a multitude of voices—angry, triumphant, scornful with an occasional oath or epithet of contempt—but the voice of Sam Houston was not heard."

At the appointed hour, the Convention clerk was instructed to call the roll of state officials. Silence settled over the vast audience, and every eye peered anxiously for a glimpse of the old hero.

"Sam Houston!" There was no response.

"Sam Houston! Sam Houston!" The rumbling and contemptuous voices began again. The office of Governor of Texas, Confederate States of America, was declared to be officially vacant; and Lieutenant Governor Edward Clark, "an insignificant creature, contemptible, spry and pert," stepped up to take the oath. (A close personal and political friend elected on Houston's ticket, Clark would later enter the executive office to demand the archives of the state, only to have his former mentor wheel slowly in his chair to face him with the grandly scornful question: "And what is your name, sir?")

In another part of the Capitol, the hero of San Jacinto, casting aside a lifetime of political fortune, fame and devotion from his people, was scrawling out his last message as Governor with a broken heart:

Fellow Citizens, in the name of your rights and liberty, which I believe have been trampled upon, I refuse to take this oath. In the name of my own conscience and my own manhood . . . I refuse to take this oath. . . . [But] I love Texas too well to bring civil strife and bloodshed upon her. I shall make no endeavor to maintain my authority as Chief Executive of this state, except by the peaceful exercise of my functions. When I can no longer do this, I shall calmly withdraw from the scene. . . . I am . . .

stricken down because I will not yield those principles which I have fought for. . . . The severest pang is that the blow comes in the name of the state of Texas.

PART THREE

THE TIME AND THE PLACE

THE END of the costly military struggle between North and South did not restore peace and unity on the political front. Appomattox had ended the shooting of brother by brother; but it did not halt the political invasions, the economic plundering and the intersectional hatred that still racked a divided land. The bitter animosities on both sides of the Mason-Dixon line which had engulfed Daniel Webster, Thomas Hart Benton and Sam Houston continued unabated for some two decades after the war.

But gradually, the old conflicts over emancipation and reconstruction faded away, and exploitation of the newly opened West and the trampled South brought new issues and new faces to the Senate. It was no longer the forum for our greatest Constitutional lawyers, for Constitutional issues no longer dominated American public life. Easy money, sudden fortunes, increasingly powerful political machines and blatant corruption transformed much of the nation; and the Senate, as befits a democratic legislative body, accurately represented the nation. Corporation lawyers and political bosses, not constitutional orators, were the spokesmen for this roaring era; although too many of the nation's talented men found fame and fortune more readily available in the world of high finance and industry, rather than the seemingly dull and unnoticed labors of government. (If Daniel Webster had lived in that age, one editor commented, he would have been "neither in debt nor in the Senate.") Eleven new states were added quickly as the West was developed; and twenty-two new Senators and a tremendous new chamber detracted from that old distinctive atmosphere. Sectionalism, logrolling and a series of near-fanatical movements—of which the "free silver" movement that embroiled Lamar was only the beginning —plagued Senate deliberations on domestic economic issues.

Senators, said William Allen White, represented not only states and regions but "principalities and powers and businesses":

> One Senator, for instance, represented the Union Pacific Railway System, another the New York Central, still another the insurance interests. . . . Coal and iron owned a coterie . . . cotton had half a dozen Senators. And so it went. . . . It was a plutocratic feudalism . . . eminently respectable. The collar of any great financial interest was worn in pride.

Thus by the end of the nineteenth century the Senate had come to very nearly its lowest ebb, in terms of power as well as prestige. The decline in Senatorial power had begun shortly after the end of Grant's administration. Prior to that time, the Senate, which had humiliated President Johnson and dominated President Grant, had reigned supreme in what was very nearly a parliamentary form of government. But the peak of Congressional power passed as Presidents Hayes, Garfield, Arthur and Cleveland successfully resisted Senatorial attempts to dictate Presidential appointments, and the government returned to the more traditional American system of the Constitution's checks and balances.

The decline in the Senate's power, moreover, had been foreshadowed by a rapid decline in prestige even before economic issues had replaced the sectional and constitutional conflict. British and Canadian diplomats maintained that they had secured approval of the Reciprocity Treaty of 1854 by seeing to it that it was "floated through on waves of champagne. . . . If you have got to deal with hogs, what are you to do?"

But the Senate, despite its decline in power and public esteem during the second half of the nineteenth century, did not consist entirely of hogs. It still contained men worthy of respect, and men of courage. Of these, Edmund Ross and those who stood with him in the Johnson impeachment trial selflessly sacrificed themselves to save the nation from reckless abuse of legislative power. And Lucius Lamar, by his gentle but firm determination to be a statesman, was instrumental in reuniting the nation in preparation for the new challenges which lay ahead.

FIVE

EDMUND G. ROSS

"I looked down into my open grave . . ."

In a lonely grave, forgotten and unknown, lies "the man who saved a President," and who as a result may well have preserved for ourselves and posterity constitutional government in the United States—the man who performed in 1868 what one historian has called "the most heroic act in American history, incomparably more difficult than any deed of valor upon the field of battle"—but a United States Senator whose name no one recalls: Edmund G. Ross of Kansas.

The impeachment of President Andrew Johnson, the event in which the obscure Ross was to play such a dramatic role, was the sensational climax to the bitter struggle between the President, determined to carry out Abraham Lincoln's policies of reconciliation with the defeated South, and the more radical Republican leaders in Congress, who sought to administer the downtrodden Southern states as conquered provinces which had forfeited their rights under the Constitution. It

84

was, moreover, a struggle between Executive and Legislative authority. Andrew Johnson, the courageous if untactful Tennessean who had been the only Southern Member of Congress to refuse to secede with his state, had committed himself to the policies of the Great Emancipator to whose high station he had succeeded only by the course of an assassin's bullet. He knew that Lincoln prior to his death had already clashed with the extremists in Congress, who had opposed his approach to reconstruction in a constitutional and charitable manner and sought to make the Legislative Branch of the government supreme. And his own belligerent temperament soon destroyed any hope that Congress might now join hands in carrying out Lincoln's policies of permitting the South to resume its place in the Union with as little delay and controversy as possible.

By 1866, when Edmund Ross first came to the Senate, the two branches of the government were already at each other's throats, snarling and bristling with anger. Bill after bill was vetoed by the President on the grounds that they were unconstitutional, too harsh in their treatment of the South, an unnecessary prolongation of military rule in peacetime or undue interference with the authority of the Executive Branch. And for the first time in our nation's history, important public measures were passed over a President's veto and became law without his support.

But not all of Andrew Johnson's vetoes were overturned; and the "Radical" Republicans of the Congress promptly realized that one final step was necessary before they could crush their despised foe (and in the heat of political battle their vengeance was turned upon their President far more than their former military enemies of the South). That one remaining step was the assurance of a two-thirds majority in the Senate—for under the Constitution, such a majority was necessary to override a Presidential veto. And more important, such a majority was constitutionally required to accomplish their major ambition, now an ill-kept secret, conviction of the President under an impeachment and his dismissal from office!

The temporary and unstable two-thirds majority which had enabled the Senate Radical Republicans on several occasions to enact legislation over the President's veto was, they knew, insufficiently reliable for an impeachment conviction. To solidify this bloc became the paramount goal of Congress, expressly or impliedly governing its decisions on other issues—particularly the admission of new states, the readmission of Southern

states and the determination of senatorial cre-
dentials. By extremely dubious methods a pro-
Johnson Senator was denied his seat. Over the
President's veto Nebraska was admitted to the
Union, seating two more anti-administration Senators. Although last-minute maneuvers failed to
admit Colorado over the President's veto (sparsely
populated Colorado had rejected statehood in a
referendum), an unexpected tragedy brought
false tears and fresh hopes for a new vote, in
Kansas.

Senator Jim Lane of Kansas had been a "conservative" Republican sympathetic to Johnson's
plans to carry out Lincoln's reconstruction policies. But his frontier state was one of the most
"radical" in the Union. When Lane voted to up-
hold Johnson's veto of the Civil Rights Bill of 1866
and introduced the administration's bill for recognition of the new state government of Arkansas,
Kansas had arisen in outraged heat. A mass meeting at Lawrence had vilified the Senator and
speedily reported resolutions sharply condemning
his position. Humiliated, mentally ailing, broken
in health and laboring under charges of financial
irregularities, Jim Lane took his own life on July
1, 1866.

With this thorn in their side removed, the Radi-

Ross condemns Lane at the Lawrence meeting.

cal Republicans in Washington looked anxiously toward Kansas and the selection of Lane's successor. Their fondest hopes were realized, for the new Senator from Kansas turned out to be Edmund G. Ross, the very man who had introduced the resolutions attacking Lane at Lawrence.

There could be no doubt as to where Ross's sympathies lay, for his entire career was one of determined opposition to the slave states of the South, their practices and their friends.

The stage was now set for the final scene—the removal of Johnson. Early in 1867, Congress enacted over the President's veto the Tenure-of-Office Bill which prevented the President from removing without the consent of the Senate all new officeholders whose appointment required confirmation by that body. At the time nothing more than the cry for more patronage was involved, Cabinet Members having originally been specifically exempt.

On August 5, 1867, President Johnson—convinced that the Secretary of War, whom he had inherited from Lincoln, Edwin M. Stanton, was the surreptitious tool of the Radical Republicans and was seeking to become the almighty dictator of the conquered South—asked for his immediate resignation; and Stanton arrogantly fired back the reply that he declined to resign before the next meeting of Congress. Not one to cower before this kind of effrontery, the President one week later suspended Stanton, and appointed in his place the one man whom Stanton did not dare resist, General Grant. On January 13, 1868, an angry Senate notified the President and Grant that it did not concur in the suspension of Stanton, and Grant vacated the office upon Stanton's return. But the situation was intolerable. The Secretary of War was unable to attend Cabinet meetings or associate with his colleagues in the administration; and on February 21, President Johnson, anxious to obtain a court test of the act he believed obviously unconstitutional, again notified Stanton that he had been summarily removed from the office of Secretary of War.

While Stanton, refusing to yield possession, barricaded himself in his office, public opinion in the nation ran heavily against the President. He had intentionally broken the law and dictatorially thwarted the will of Congress! Although previous resolutions of impeachment had been defeated in the House, both in committee and on the floor, a new resolution was swiftly reported and adopted on February 24 by a tremendous vote.

With the President impeached—in effect, indicted—by the House, the frenzied trial for his conviction or acquittal under the Articles of Impeachment began on March 5 in the Senate, presided over by the Chief Justice.

To each Senator the Chief Justice administered an oath "to do impartial justice" (including even the hot-headed Radical Senator from Ohio, Benjamin Wade, who as President Pro Tempore of the Senate was next in line for the Presidency). The chief prosecutor for the House was General Benjamin F. Butler, the "butcher of New Orleans," a talented but coarse and demagogic Congressman from Massachusetts. (When he lost his seat in 1874, he was so hated by his own party as well as his opponents that one Republican wired concerning the Democratic sweep, "Butler defeated, everything else lost.")

From the fifth of March to the sixteenth of May, the drama continued. Of the eleven Articles of Impeachment adopted by the House, the first eight were based upon the removal of Stanton and the appointment of a new Secretary of War in violation of the Tenure-of-Office Act; the ninth related to Johnson's conversation with a general which was said to induce violations of the Army Appropriations Act; the tenth recited that Johnson had delivered "intemperate, inflammatory and scandalous harangues . . . as well against Congress as the laws of the United States"; and the eleventh was a deliberately obscure conglomeration of all the charges in the preceding articles.

As the trial progressed, it became increasingly apparent that the impatient Republicans did not intend to give the President a fair trial on the formal issues upon which the impeachment was drawn, but intended instead to depose him from the White House on any grounds, real or imagined, for refusing to accept their policies. Telling evidence in the President's favor was arbitrarily excluded. Prejudgment on the part of most Senators was brazenly announced. Attempted bribery and other forms of pressure were rampant. The chief interest was not in the trial or the evidence, but in the tallying of votes necessary for conviction.

Twenty-seven states (excluding the unrecognized Southern states) in the Union meant fifty-four members of the Senate, and thirty-six votes were required to constitute the two-thirds majority necessary for conviction. All twelve Democratic votes were obviously lost, and the forty-two Republicans knew that they could afford to lose only six of their own members if Johnson were to be ousted. To their dismay, at a preliminary Republican caucus, six courageous Republicans indicated that the evidence so far introduced was not in their opinion sufficient to convict Johnson under the Articles of Impeachment. "Infamy!" cried the Philadelphia *Press*. The Republic has "been betrayed in the house of its friends!"

But if the remaining thirty-six Republicans would hold, there would be no doubt as to the outcome. All must stand together! But one Republican Senator would not announce his verdict in the preliminary poll—Edmund G. Ross of Kansas.

The Republicans insisted that Ross's crucial vote was rightfully theirs, and they were determined to get it by whatever means available. As stated by DeWitt in his memorable *Impeachment of Andrew Johnson*, "The full brunt of the struggle turned at last on the one remaining doubtful Senator, Edmund G. Ross."

When the impeachment resolution had passed the House, Senator Ross had casually remarked to Senator Sprague of Rhode Island, "Well, Sprague, the thing is here; and, so far as I am concerned, though a Republican and opposed to Mr. Johnson and his policy, he shall have as fair a trial as an accused man ever had on this earth." Immediately the word spread that "Ross was shaky." "From that hour," he later wrote, "not a day passed that did not bring me, by mail and telegraph and in personal intercourse, appeals to stand fast for impeachment, and not a few were the admonitions of condign visitations upon any indication even of lukewarmness."

Ross and his fellow doubtful Republicans were daily pestered, spied upon and subjected to every form of pressure. Their residences were carefully watched, their social circles suspiciously scrutinized, and their every move and companions secretly marked in special notebooks. They were warned in the party press, harangued by their constituents, and sent dire warnings threatening political ostracism and even assassination.

The New York *Tribune* reported that Edmund Ross in particular was "mercilessly dragged this way and that by both sides, hunted like a fox night and day and badgered by his own colleagues, like the bridge at Arcola now trod upon by one Army and now trampled by the other." His background and life were investigated from top to bottom, and his constituents and colleagues pursued him throughout Washington to gain some inkling of his opinion. He was the target of every eye, his name was on every mouth and his intentions were discussed in every newspaper. Although there is evidence that he gave some hint of agreement to

each side, and each attempted to claim him publicly, he actually kept both sides in a state of complete suspense by his judicial silence.

The night before the Senate was to take its first
vote for the conviction or acquittal of Johnson,
Ross received this telegram from home:

> Kansas has heard the evidence and demands the
> conviction of the President.
>> (*signed*) D. R. ANTHONY AND 1,000 OTHERS

And on that fateful morning of May 16 Ross replied:

> To D. R. Anthony and 1,000 Others: I do not
> recognize your right to demand that I vote either for
> or against conviction. I have taken an oath to do
> impartial justice according to the Constitution and
> laws, and trust that I shall have the courage to vote
> according to the dictates of my judgment and for
> the highest good of the country.
>> [signed]—E. G. ROSS

That morning spies traced Ross to his breakfast;
and ten minutes before the vote was taken his
Kansas colleague warned him in the presence of
Thaddeus Stevens that a vote for acquittal would
mean trumped up charges and his political death.

But now the fateful hour was at hand. Neither
escape, delay or indecision was possible. As Ross

himself later described it: "The galleries were packed. Tickets of admission were at an enormou premium. The House had adjourned and all of it members were in the Senate chamber. Every chai on the Senate floor was filled with a Senator, a Cabinet Officer, a member of the President's coun sel or a member of the House." Every Senator wa in his seat, the desperately ill Grimes of Iowa being literally carried in.

It had been decided to take the first vote unde that broad Eleventh Article of Impeachment, be lieved to command the widest support. As the Chief Justice announced the voting would begin he reminded "the citizens and strangers in the galleries that absolute silence and perfect orde are required." But already a deathlike stillnes. enveloped the Senate chamber. A Congressmar later recalled that "Some of the members of the House near me grew pale and sick under the burden of suspense"; and Ross noted that there was even "a subsidence of the shuffling of feet, the rustling of silks, the fluttering of fans, and of con versation."

The voting tensely commenced. By the time the Chief Justice reached the name of Edmund Ross twenty-four "guilties" had been pronounced. Ter more were certain and one other practically cer ain. Only Ross's vote was needed to obtain the hirty-six votes necessary to convict the President. 3ut not a single person in the room knew how this young Kansan would vote. Unable to conceal the suspense and emotion in his voice, the Chief Justice put the question to him: "Mr. Senator Ross, now say you? Is the respondent Andrew Johnson guilty or not guilty of a high misdemeanor as charged in this Article?" Every voice was still; every eye was upon the freshman Senator from Kansas. The hopes and fears, the hatred and bitterness of past decades were centered upon this one man.

As Ross himself later described it,

I almost literally looked down into my open grave. Friendships, position, fortune, everything that makes life desirable to an ambitious man were about to be swept away by the breath of my mouth, perhaps forever.

Then came the answer again in a voice that could not be misunderstood—full, final, definite, unhesitating and unmistakable: "Not guilty." The deed was done, the President saved, the trial as good as over and the conviction lost.

A ten-day recess followed, ten turbulent days to change votes on the remaining Articles. An attempt was made to rush through bills to readmit six Southern states, whose twelve Senators were guaranteed to vote for conviction. But this could not be accomplished in time. Again Ross was the only one uncommitted on the other Articles, the only one whose vote could not be predicted in advance. And again he was subjected to terrible pressure. From "D. R. Anthony and others," he received a wire informing him that "Kansas repudiates you as she does all perjurers and skunks."

Again the wild rumors spread that Ross had been won over on the remaining Articles of Impeachment. As the Senate reassembled, he was the only one of the seven "renegade" Republicans to vote with the majority on preliminary procedural matters. But when the second and third Articles of Impeachment were read, and the name of Ross was reached again with the same intense suspense of ten days earlier, again came the calm answer "Not guilty."

Why did Ross, whose dislike for Johnson continued, vote "Not guilty"? His motives appear clearly from his own writings on the subject years later in articles contributed to *Scribner's* and *Forum* magazines:

> In a large sense, the independence of the executive office as a coordinate branch of the government was on trial. . . . If . . . the President must step down

... a disgraced man and a political outcast ... upon insufficient proofs and from partisan considerations, the office of President would be degraded, cease to be a coordinate branch of the government, and ever after subordinated to the legislative will. It would practically have revolutionized our splendid political fabric into a partisan Congressional autocracy. ... This government had never faced so insidious a danger ... control by the worst element of American politics. ... If Andrew Johnson were acquitted by a nonpartisan vote ... America would pass the danger point of partisan rule and that intolerance which so often characterizes the sway of great majorities and makes them dangerous.

Neither Ross nor any other Republican who had voted for the acquittal of Johnson was ever reelected to the Senate, not a one of them retaining the support of their party's organization. When he returned to Kansas in 1871, he and his family suffered social ostracism, physical attack, and near poverty.

Who was Edmund G. Ross? Practically nobody. Not a single public law bears his name, not a single history book includes his picture, not a single list of Senate "greats" mentions his service. His one heroic deed has been all but forgotten. But who might Edmund G. Ross have been? That is the question—for Ross, a man with an excellent command of words, an excellent background for politics and an excellent future in the Senate might well have outstripped his colleagues in prestige and power throughout a long Senate career. Instead, he chose to throw all of this away for one act of conscience.

I could not close the story of Edmund Ross without some more adequate mention of those six courageous Republicans who stood with Ross and braved denunciation to acquit Andrew Johnson. Edmund Ross, more than any of those six colleagues, endured more before and after his vote, reached his conscientious decision with greater difficulty, and aroused the greatest interest and suspense prior to May 16 by his noncommittal silence. His story, like his vote, is the key to the impeachment tragedy. But all seven of the Republicans who voted against conviction should be remembered for their courage. Not a single one of them ever won re-election to the Senate. Not a single one of them escaped the unholy combination of threats, bribes and coercive tactics by which their fellow Republicans attempted to intimidate their votes; and not a single one of them escaped the terrible torture of vicious criticism engendered by their vote to acquit.

William Pitt Fessenden of Maine, one of the most eminent Senators, orators and lawyers of his day, and a prominent senior Republican leader, who admired Stanton and disliked Johnson, became convinced early in the game that "the whole thing is a mere madness."

John B. Henderson of Missouri, one of the Senate's

youngest members, had previously demonstrated high courage by introducing the Thirteenth Amendment abolishing slavery, simply because he was convinced that it would pass only if sponsored by a slave-state Senator, whose political death would necessarily follow.

Peter Van Winkle of West Virginia, the last doubtful Republican name to be called on May 16, was, like Ross, a "nobody"; but his firm "not guilty" extinguished the last faint glimmer of hope which Edmund Ross had already all but destroyed.

The veteran Lyman Trumbull of Illinois, who had defeated Abe Lincoln for the Senate, had drafted much of the major reconstruction legislation which Johnson vetoed, and had voted to censure Johnson upon Stanton's removal.

But, in the eyes of the Philadelphia *Press,* his "statesmanship drivelled into selfishness," for, resisting tremendous pressure, he voted against conviction.

Joseph Smith Fowler of Tennessee, like Ross, Henderson, and Van Winkle a freshman Senator, at first thought the President impeachable. But the former Nashville professor was horrified by the mad passion of the House in rushing through the impeachment resolution by evidence against Johnson "based on falsehood," and by the "corrupt and dishonorable" Ben Butler, "a wicked man who seeks to convert the Senate of the United States into a political guillotine."

James W. Grimes was a man of great physical as well as moral courage, and just before the balloting was to begin on May 16, four men carried the pale and withered Senator from Iowa into his seat. He later wrote that

Fessenden had grasped his hand and given him a "glori-
fied smile. . . . I would not today exchange that recollec-
tion for the highest distinction of life." The Chief Justice
suggested that it would be permissible for him to remain
seated while voting—but with the assistance of his
friends, Senator Grimes struggled to his feet and in a
surprisingly firm voice called out "not guilty."

LUCIUS QUINTUS CINCINNATUS LAMAR

"Today I must be true or false . . ."

NO ONE HAD EVER SEEN that hardened veteran politician, Speaker of the House James G. Blaine, cry. But there he sat, with the tears streaming unashamedly down his cheeks, unable to conceal his emotions from the full view of the House members and spectators. But few on the floor or in the galleries on that dramatic day in 1874 were paying much attention to Mr. Blaine, and most were making no attempt to hide their own tears. Democrats and Republicans alike, battle-scarred veterans of the Civil War and the violence of politics, sat in somber silence, as they listened to the urgent entreaties of the Freshman Congressman from Mississippi. Speaking simply and clearly, without resorting to the customary rhetorical devices, his full, rich voice touched the hearts of every listener with its simple plea for amity and justice between North and South.

All were touched, yes, by his message; but stunned, too, by its impact—for Lucius Lamar of Mississippi was appealing in the name of the South's most implacable enemy, the Radical Republican who had helped make the Reconstruction Period a black nightmare the South never could forget: Charles Sumner of Massachusetts. Charles Sumner—who assailed Daniel Webster as a traitor for seeking to keep the South in the Union —who helped crucify Edmund Ross for his vote against the Congressional mob rule that would have ground the South and the Presidency under its heel—whose own death was hastened by the terrible caning administered to him on the Senate floor years earlier by Congressman Brooks of South Carolina, who thereupon became a Southern hero—Charles Sumner was now dead. And Lucius Lamar, known in the prewar days as one of the most rabid "fire-eaters" ever to come out of the deep South, was standing on the floor of the House and delivering a moving eulogy lamenting his departure!

Few speeches in American political history have had such immediate impact. Overnight it raised Lamar to the first rank in the Congress and in the country; and more importantly it marked a

Lamar fought bravely for the Confederacy.

turning point in the relations between North and South.

Southerners to whom Charles Sumner symbolized the worst of the prewar abolitionist movement and the postwar reconstruction felt betrayed. Several leading Mississippi newspapers, including the Columbus *Democrat*, the Canton *Mail* and the Meridian *Mercury*, vigorously criticized Lamar, as did many of his old friends, maintaining that he had surrendered Southern principle and honor.

Such attacks, however, were in the minority. It was generally recognized, North and South, that the speech which could have been a disaster was in fact a notable triumph. It was obvious that moved by the strange forces of history and personal destiny, the man and the occasion had met that day in Washington.

Mississippians, on the whole, came either to understand and admire the sentiments of the Sumner eulogy, to respect Lamar's sincerity if they did not admire it, or to forgive him for what they considered to be one serious error of judgment if they were strongly opposed to it. Riding a wave of popularity and the 1876 return to Democratic rule in Mississippi, Lamar was elected by the legislature to the United States Senate. But even before he moved from the House to the Senate, Lamar again outraged many of his backers by abandoning his party and section on another heated issue.

The Hayes-Tilden Presidential contest of 1876 had been a bitter struggle, apparently culminating in a close electoral-vote victory for the Democrat Tilden. Although Hayes at first accepted his defeat with philosophic resignation, his lieutenants, with the cooperation of the Republican *New York Times*, converted the apparent certainty of Tilden's election into doubt by claiming the closely contested states of South Carolina, Louisiana and Florida—and then attempted to convert that doubt into the certainty of Hayes' election by procuring from the carpetbag governments of those three states doctored election returns. With rumors of violence and military dictatorship rife, Congress determined upon arbitration by a supposedly nonpartisan Electoral Commission—and Lucius Lamar, confident that an objective inquiry would demonstrate the palpable fraud of the Republican case, agreed to this solution to prevent a recurrence of the tragic conflict which had so aged his spirit and broadened his outlook.

But when the Commission, acting wholly along party lines, awarded the disputed states and the election to Hayes with 185 electoral votes to 184 for Tilden, the South was outraged. Four more years of Republican rule meant four more years of Southern bondage and exploitation, four more years before the South could regain her dignity and her rightful place in the nation. Lamar was accused of trading his vote and his section's honor for a promise of a future position; he was accused of cowardice, of being afraid to stand up for his

state when it meant a fight; and he was accused of
deserting his people and his party in the very hour
when triumph should have been at last rightfully
theirs. His enemies, realizing that six years would
pass before Senator-elect Lamar would be forced
to run for re-election, vowed never to forget that
day of perfidy.

But Lucius Lamar, a man of law and honor,
could not now repudiate the findings, however
shocking, of the Commission he had helped establish. He supported the findings of the Commission
because he believed that only force could prevent
Hayes' inauguration and that it would be disastrous
to travel that road again. It was better, he believed, for the South—in spite of provocation—to
accept defeat on this occasion. He was skillful
enough, however, to get Hayes committed to concessions for the South, including the withdrawal of
military occupation forces and a return to Home
Rule in key states.

As Senator Lamar, ill and fatigued, rested at
home throughout much of 1877, a new movement
was sweeping the South and West, a movement
which would plague the political parties of the
nation for a generation to come—"free silver." The
Moses of the silver forces, William Jennings
Bryan, had not yet appeared on the scene; but

"Silver Dick" Bland, the Democratic Representative from Missouri, was leading the way with his bill for the free coinage of all silver brought to the Mint. Inasmuch as a tremendous spurt in the production of the western silver mines had caused its value in relation to gold to shrink considerably, the single purpose of the silver forces was clear, simple and appealing—easy, inflationary money.

It was a tremendously popular cause in Mississippi. The panic of 1873 had engulfed the nation into the most terrible depression it had ever suffered, and the already impoverished states of the South were particularly hard hit. Businesses failed by the thousands, unemployment increased and wages were reduced. Farm prices dropped rapidly from their high wartime levels and the farmers of Mississippi—desperate for cash—vowed support of any bill which would raise the price of their commodities, lower the value of their debts, and increase the availability of money. The South foresaw itself in a state of permanent indebtedness to the financial institutions of the East unless easy money could be made available to pay its heavy debts.

But Lamar, the learned scholar and professor, approached the issue somewhat differently than his colleagues. Paying but little heed to the demands of his constituents, he exhausted all available treatises on both sides of the controversy. His study convinced him—possibly wrongly—that the only sound position was in support of sound money. The payment of our government's debts—even to the "bloated bondholders" of Wall Street—in a debased, inflated currency, as the Bland Bill encouraged and the accompanying Matthews Resolution specifically provided, was an ethical wrong and a practical mistake, he felt, certain to embarrass our standing in the eyes of the world, and promoted not as a permanent financial program but as a spurious relief bill to alleviate the nation's economic distress.

On January 24, 1878, in a courageous and learned address—his first major speech on the Senate floor—Lamar rejected the pleas of Mississippi voters and assailed elaborate rationalizations behind the two silver measures as artificial and exaggerated. And the following day he voted "No" on the Matthews Resolution, in opposition to his colleague from Mississippi, a Negro Republican of exceptional talents elected several years earlier by the old "carpetbag" Legislature.

Praise for Senator Lamar's masterly and statesmanlike analysis of the issue emanated from many parts of the country, but from Mississippi came little but condemnation. On January 30, the State Legislature adopted a Memorial omitting all mention of Lamar but—in an obvious and deliberate slap—congratulating and thanking his colleague (to whom the white Democratic legislators normally were bitterly opposed) for voting the opposite way and thus reflecting "the sentiment and will of his constituents." The Memorial deeply hurt Lamar, and he was little consoled by a letter from his close friend, the Speaker of the Mississippi House, who termed it "a damned outrage" but explained:

> The people are under a pressure of hard times and scarcity of money, and their representatives felt bound to strike at something which might give relief, the how or wherefor very few of them could explain.

But the Legislature was not through. On February 4, a resolution was passed by both Houses instructing Lamar to vote for the Bland Silver Bill, and to use his efforts as spokesman for Mississippi to secure its passage.

One week later, the Bland Silver Bill came before the Senate for a final vote. As the debate neared its end, Senator Lamar rose unexpectedly to his feet. No notes were in his hand, for he was one of the most brilliant extemporaneous speakers ever to sit in the Senate. ("The pen is an extinguisher upon my mind," he said, "and a torture to my nerves.") Instead he held an official document which bore the great seal of the State of Mississippi, and this he dispatched by page to the desk. With apologies to his colleagues, Senator Lamar explained that, although he had already expressed his views on the Silver Bill, he had "one other duty to perform; a very painful one, but one which is nonetheless clear." He then asked that the resolutions which he had sent to the desk be read.

The Senate was first astonished and then attentively silent as the Clerk droned the express will of the Mississippi Legislature that its Senators vote for the Bland Silver Bill. As the Clerk completed the instructions, all eyes turned toward Lamar, no one certain what to expect. As the reporter for the Washington *Capitol* described it:

> Remembering the embarrassing position of this gentleman with respect to the pending bill, every Senator immediately gave his attention, and the Chamber became as silent as the tomb.

A massive but lonely figure on the Senate floor, Lucius Lamar spoke in a quiet yet powerful voice, a voice which "grew tremulous with emotion, as his body fairly shook with agitation":

MR. PRESIDENT: Between these resolutions and my convictions there is a great gulf. I cannot pass it. . . . Upon the youth of my state whom it has been my privilege to assist in education I have always endeavored to impress the belief that truth was better than falsehood, honesty better than policy, courage better than cowardice. Today my lessons confront me. Today I must be true or false, honest or cunning, faithful or unfaithful to my people. Even in this hour of their legislative displeasure and disapprobation, I cannot vote as these resolutions direct.

My reasons for my vote shall be given to my people. Then it will be for them to determine if adherence to my honest convictions has disqualified me from representing them.

Senators on both sides of the bill immediately crowded about his desk to commend his courage. Lamar knew that his speech and vote could not prevent passage of the Bland Bill by a tremendous margin, and its subsequent enactment over the veto of President Hayes. Yet his intentional and stunningly courageous disobedience to the will of his constituents was not wholly in vain. Throughout the North the speech was highly praised. Distrust toward the South, and suspicion of its attitude toward the national debt and national credit, diminished. *Harper's Weekly,*

Senators on both sides crowd about Lamar's desk.

pointing out that Lamar voted in opposition to "the strong and general public feeling of his state," concluded:

> No Senator has shown himself more worthy of universal respect than Mr. Lamar; for none has stood more manfully by his principles, in the face of the most authoritative remonstrance from his state. . . . The Democratic Senator from Mississippi has

shown the manly courage which becomes an American statesman.

The Nation editorialized that the brief speech of Lucius Lamar in explanation of his disregard for the instructions of his state, "for manliness, dignity and pathos has never been surpassed in Congress. His vote will probably cost him his seat."

But like his famous uncle, Mirabeau Lamar of Texas, and other members of his family, Lucius Quintus Cincinnatus Lamar was not afraid of overwhelming odds. Admittedly he had violated the instructions of the Legislature, he said. "I will appeal to the sovereign people, the masters of the legislature who undertake to instruct me."

With this declaration, Senator Lamar launched successive tours of Mississippi. Speaking to thousands of people in crowded halls and open fields, Lamar stated frankly that he was well aware that he had not pleased his constituents; that he was equally well aware that the easier path was to exploit that sectional cause to which he had always been devoted; but that it was his intention to help create a feeling of confidence and mutuality between North and South by voting in the national interest without regard to sectional pressures.

For three or four hours at a time, his passionate and imaginative oratory held spellbound the crowds that came to jeer. "He spoke like the mountain torrent," as several observers later described it, "sweeping away the boulders in the stream that attempted to oppose his course."

But Lamar did not employ oratorical tricks to sway emotions while dodging issues. On the contrary, his speeches were a learned explanation of his position, setting forth the Constitutional history of the Senate and its relationship to the state legislatures, and the statements and examples of Burke, and of Calhoun, Webster, and other famous Senators who had disagreed with Legislative instructions: "Better to follow the example of the illustrious men whose names have been given than to abandon altogether judgment and conviction in deference to popular clamor."

His tour was tremendously successful. "Men who were so hostile that they could hardly be persuaded to hear him at all would mount upon the benches and tables, swinging their hats, and huzzaing until hoarse." Others departed in silence, weighing the significance of his words. When he spoke in Yazoo County, the stronghold of his opposition, the Yazoo City *Herald* reported that like "the lion at bay," he "conquered the prejudices of

hundreds who had been led to believe that his
views on certain points were better adapted to
the latitude of New England than to that of Mississippi." And shortly thereafter, the Yazoo Democratic County Convention adopted a resolution
that their legislators should "vote for him and
work for him, first, last, and all the time, as the
choice of this people for United States Senator."

It is heartening to note that the people of Mississippi continued their support of him, in spite
of the fact that on three important occasions—in
his eulogy of Charles Sumner in his support of the
Electoral Commission which brought about the
election of the Republican Hayes and in his exception to their strongly felt stand for free silver—
Lamar had stood against their immediate wishes.
The voters responded to the sincerity and courage
which he had shown; and they continued to give
him their support and affection throughout the
remainder of his political life. He was re-elected to
the Senate by an overwhelming majority, later to
become Chairman of the Senate Democratic
Caucus, then Secretary of the Interior and finally
Justice of the Supreme Court of the United States.
At no time did he, who has properly been termed
the most gifted statesman given by the South to
the nation from the close of the Civil War to the

turn of the century, ever veer from the deep conviction he had expressed while under bitter attack
in 1878:

> The liberty of this country and its great interests
> will never be secure if its public men become mere
> menials to do the biddings of their constituents in-
> stead of being representatives in the true sense of
> the word, looking to the lasting prosperity and
> future interests of the whole country.

PART FOUR

THE TIME AND THE PLACE

Two MEN of integrity—both Republicans, both Mid-
westerners, but wholly dissimilar in their political philoso-
phies and personal mannerisms—best illustrate the
impact of the twentieth century upon the Senate as a
whole and the atmosphere of political courage in particular. George W. Norris and Robert A. Taft, whose
careers in the Senate overlapped for only a brief period
some seventeen years ago, were masters of the legislative
process, leaders of fundamentally opposed political fac-
tions, and expounders, each in his own way, of great
constitutional doctrines. And not among the least of their
accomplishments was the increased prestige and respect
which they and others like them brought to the United
States Senate. For, at the turn of the century, the route
to fame and power for men of ability and talent had been
in industry, not in politics. And as a result, the attitude
of the public toward the political profession had too
often been characterized by apathy, indifference, disre-
spect and even amusement.

The Senate had shared in the political profession's loss
of prestige. It was due in part to the public reaction to
the new type of legislator who too often, in 1900, in-

cluded the swollen corporation lawyer and the squalid political boss. The Senate seemed to have little of the excitement and drama that had been so much a part of its existence in the years leading up to the Civil War, little of the power and prestige which it wielded so brazenly in the days of the Johnson and Grant administrations. It was in part a reaction to the increasing complexity and multiplicity of legislative issues—even Santo Domingo seemed much farther away than Fort Sumter (for blocking his Santo Domingo treaty, the Senate was told by Teddy Roosevelt that it was "wholly incompetent"), and "interstate commerce" seemed much less exciting and promising than "free silver." No longer were the names of famous Senators familiar household words, as in the days of the great triumvirate. No longer did the entire nation breathlessly follow Senate debates, as in the days of the Great Compromise or the Johnson impeachment. The nation's brightest schoolboys, who sixty or seventy years earlier would have memorized Webster's reply to Hayne, were no longer interested in politics as a career.

Those citizens who did take an active interest in the conduct of the Senate as the twentieth century got under way generally viewed it more with alarm than with pride. Throughout the nation there arose a remarkable array of reformers, muckrakers and good government movements, represented in the Senate by a new breed of idealists and independents, men of ability and statesmanship who would have ranged with the more famous names of an earlier day. To arrest the dual trends of an electorate indifferent to their Senators and Senators indifferent to their electorate, the reformers, both in and out of the Senate, finally accomplished a long overdue change in the election machinery—the power of electing Senators was taken from the legislatures of the states and given directly to the people.

There was (and is) no way of measuring statistically or scientifically the effect of the direct election of Senators on the quality of the Senate itself. There has been no scarcity of either contemptuous criticism or lavish praise for both the Senate as a whole and individual Senators. But too often such judgments consist of generalizations from limited cases or experiences. Woodrow Wilson, for example, shortly before his death, buffeted by the Senate in his efforts on behalf of the League of Nations and the Versailles Treaty, rejected the suggestion that he seek a seat in the Senate from New Jersey, stating: "Outside of the United States, the Senate does not amount to a damn. And inside the United States the Senate is mostly despised; they haven't had a thought down there in fifty years." There are many who agreed with Wilson in 1920, and some who might agree with those sentiments today.

But Professor Woodrow Wilson, prior to his baptism of political fire, had regarded the Senate as one of the ablest and most powerful legislative bodies in the world. In part this power, and the ability it required in those Senators who sought to harness it, sprang from the growing influence of Federal legislation in domestic affairs. But even more important was the Senate's gradually increasing power in the field of foreign affairs—a power which multiplied as our nation's stature in the com-

munity of nations grew, a power which made the Senate
in the twentieth century a far more significant body, in
terms of the actual consequences of its decisions, than
the glittering Senate of Webster, Clay and Calhoun,
which had toiled endlessly but fruitlessly over the slavery question.

And just as a nation torn by internal crisis had demanded Senators of courage in 1850, so did a nation
plunged into international crisis. John Quincy Adams
had realized this one hundred years before George
Norris ever came to Washington. But he could not have
foreseen that this nation's role in the world would bring
constantly recurring crises and troublesome problems to
the floor of the United States Senate, crises which would
force men like George Norris to choose between conscience and constituents, problems which would force
men like Bob Taft to choose between principles and
popularity.

These are not the only stories of political courage in
the twentieth century, possibly not even the most outstanding or significant. Yet the changing nature of the
Senate, its work and its members, seems to have lessened
the frequency with which the nation is given inspiration
by a selfless stand for great but unpopular principles.
Perhaps we are still too close in time to those in our
own midst whose actions a more detached historical perspective may someday stamp as worthy of recording in
the annals of political courage.

GEORGE NORRIS

"I have come home to tell you the truth."

AT PRECISELY 1:00 P.M. one wintry afternoon
early in 1910, Representative John Dalzell of
Pennsylvania left the Speaker's Chair and walked
out of the House Chamber for his daily cup of
coffee and piece of pie in the Capitol restaurant.
His departure was not unusual—for Representative Dalzell, who was Speaker Joe Cannon's first
assistant in ruling the House from the Speaker's
Chair, had always left the Chamber at exactly that
hour, and he was almost invariably succeeded in
the Chair by Representative Walter Smith of
Iowa. But on that particular January afternoon
Representative Dalzell's journey up the aisle was
watched with curious satisfaction by a somewhat
shaggy looking Representative in a plain black
suit and a little shoestring tie. And the Assistant Speaker had no sooner reached the door of
the Chamber when Republican Representative
George W. Norris of Nebraska walked over to
Representative Smith and asked if he might be

recognized for two minutes. Smith, a member of
the Cannon-Dalzell Republican ruling clique but
a personal friend of Norris', agreed.

To his astonishment, Representative Norris
sought to amend the resolution then under debate
—a resolution calling for a joint committee to
investigate the Ballinger-Pinchot conservation
dispute—by requiring the entire House of Representatives to appoint its members to the investi-
gating committee, instead of granting the
customary authority to the Speaker to make such
selections.

Page boys scurried out to find Cannon and
Dalzell. This was insurrection in the ranks—the
first attempt to limit the previously unlimited
power of "Czar" Cannon! But Norris insisted that
all he desired was a fair investigation, not one
rigged by the administration. Joined by Pinchot
followers, fellow insurgent Republicans and practically all of the Democrats, he succeeded in having his amendment adopted by the narrow margin
of 149 to 146.

It was the first setback the powerful Speaker
had ever suffered, and he vowed never to forget
it. But for George Norris, the victory on the investigation resolution was only a preliminary step.
For in the inner pocket of his threadbare black

coat was a scrawled resolution which he had drafted years before—a resolution to have the House, rather than the Speaker, appoint the members of the Rules Committee itself, the Committee which completely dictated the House program and was in turn completely dominated by the Speaker.

On St. Patrick's Day in 1910, Norris rose to address the "Czar." Only minutes before, Cannon had ruled that a census bill promoted by one of his cohorts was privileged under the Constitution and could be considered out of order, inasmuch as that document provided for the taking of the census. "Mr. Speaker," called Norris, "I present a resolution made privileged by the Constitution." "The gentleman will present it," replied Cannon, smugly unaware of the attack about to be launched. And George Norris unfolded that tattered paper from his coat pocket and asked the Clerk to read it aloud.

Panic broke out in the Republican leadership. Cloakroom rumors had previously indicated the nature of Norris' proposed resolution—but it was merely a subject of contemptuous amusement among the regular Republicans, who knew they had the power to bury it forever in the Rules Committee itself. Now Cannon's own ruling on

the census bill in support of his friend had given
Norris—and his resolution, clearly based on the
Constitution's provision for House rules—an opening, an opening through which the Nebraska
Congressman led all of the insurgent and Democratic forces. Cannon and his lieutenants were
masters of parliamentary maneuvering and they
were not immediately ready to concede. They attempted to adjourn, to recess, to make a quorum
impossible. They continued debate on whether
the resolution was privileged while the party
faithful hurried back from St. Patrick's Day
parades. They kept the House in constant session
hoping to break the less organized revolters. All
night long the insurgents stayed in their seats, unwilling to nap off the floor for fear that Cannon
would suddenly rule in their absence.

Finally, all attempts at intimidation and compromise having failed, Speaker Cannon, as expected, ruled the resolution out of order; and
Norris promptly appealed the decision. By a vote
of 182 to 160, Democrats and insurgent Republicans overruled the Speaker, and by a still larger
margin Norris' resolution—already amended to
obtain Democratic support—was adopted. The
most ruthless and autocratic Speaker in the history
of the House of Representatives thereupon sub-

mitted his resignation; but George Norris, who insisted his fight was to end the dictatorial powers
of the office rather than to punish the individual,
voted against its acceptance. Years later, Cannon
was to say to him:

> Norris, throughout our bittery controversy, I do
> not recall a single instance in which you have been
> unfair. I cannot say this of many of your associates;
> and I want to say to you now that if any member of
> your damned gang had to be elected to the Senate,
> I would prefer it be you more than any of them.

The overthrow of Cannonism broke the strangle
hold which the conservative Republican leaders
had held over the Government and the nation;
and it also ended whatever favors the Representative from Nebraska had previously received at
their hands. Under the "Czar," the office of the
Speaker of the House wielded what sometimes
appeared to be very nearly equal power with the
President and the entire United States Senate. It
was a power that placed party above all other
considerations, a power that fed on party loyalty,
patronage and political organizations. It was a
power which, despite increasing disfavor in all
parts of the country outside the East, had continued unchallenged for years. But "one man without position," an editor commented, "against 200

welded into the most powerful political machine
that Washington has ever known, has twice
beaten them at their own game. Mr. George
Norris is a man worth knowing and watching."

No single chapter could recount in full all of the
courageous and independent battles led by
George Norris. His most enduring accomplishments were in the field of public power, and there
are few parallels to his long fight to bring the bene-
fits of low-cost electricity to the people of the
Tennessee Valley, although they lived a thousand
miles from his home state of Nebraska. But there
were three struggles in his life that are worthy of
especial note for the courage displayed—the overthrow of "Czar" Cannon already described; his
support of Al Smith for President in 1928; and
his filibuster against the Armed Ship Bill in 1917.

When Woodrow Wilson, sorrowfully determined upon a policy of "armed neutrality" in early
1917, appeared before a tense joint session of Congress to request legislation authorizing him to arm
American merchant ships, the American public
gave its immediate approval. Unrestricted German submarine warfare was enforcing a tight
blockade by which the Kaiser sought to starve the
British Isles into submission; and Secretary of

State Lansing had been politely informed that every American ship encountered in the war zone would be torpedoed. Already American vessels had been searched, seized and sunk. Tales of atrocities to our seamen filled the press.

As debate on the bill got under way, the newspapers learned of a new plot against the United States, contained in a message from the German Under Secretary of State for Foreign Affairs, Zimmerman, to the German Minister in Mexico. The alleged note (for there were those who questioned its authenticity and the motives of the British and American governments in disclosing it at that particular time) proposed a scheme to align Mexico and Japan against the United States. In return for its use as an invasion base, Mexico was promised restoration of her "American colonies," seized more than seventy years earlier by Sam Houston and his compatriots.

When the contents of the Zimmerman note were leaked to the newspapers, all resistance to the Armed Ship Bill in the House of Representatives instantly collapsed. The Bill was rushed through that body by the overwhelming vote of 403 to 13 —a vote which seemed clearly representative of popular opinion in favor of the President's move.

Certainly the overwhelming support given the bill by Nebraska's Congressmen represented the feelings of that state.

But in the Senate on March 2, 1917, the Armed Ship Bill met determined opposition from a small bipartisan band of insurgents led by Robert La Follette of Wisconsin and George Norris of Nebraska. As freshman Senator from a state which the previous year had voted for a Democratic legislature, Governor, Senator and President, George Norris (unlike La Follette) was neither a solidly established political figure in his own bailiwick nor confident that his people were opposed to Wilson and his policies.

In previous months he had supported the President on major foreign policy issues, including the severing of diplomatic ties with the German government. Although a militant pacifist and isolationist, his very nature prohibited him from being a mere obstructionist on all international issues, or a petty partisan opposing all of the President's requests. (Indeed, by the time World War II approached, his isolationism had largely vanished.)

But George Norris hated war—and he feared that "Big Business," which he believed was providing the stimuli for our progress along the road to war, was bent on driving the nation into a use-

ess, bloody struggle; that the President—far from
aking the people into his confidence—was trying
o stampede public opinion into pressuring the
enate for war; and that the Armed Ship Bill was
device to protect American munition profits
vith American lives, a device which could push
s directly into the conflict as a combatant with-
ut further deliberation by Congress or actual
ttack upon the United States by Germany. He
vas fearful of the bill's broad grant of authority,
nd he was resentful of the manner in which it
vas being steamrollered through the Congress. It
s not now important whether Norris was right or
vrong. What is now important is the courage he
lisplayed in support of his convictions.

"People may not believe it," Senator Norris once
aid, "but I don't like to get into fights." In 1917,
vhether he liked it or not, the freshman from
Nebraska prepared for one of the hardest, most
mbittering struggles of his political career. Since
hose days were prior to Norris' own Twentieth,
r Lame Duck, Amendment, the Sixty-fourth Con-
ress would expire at noon of March 4, when a
ew Presidential term began. Thus passage of the
ill by that Congress could be prevented if the
enate could not vote before that hour; and Norris
nd his little band were hopeful that the new

Congress, chosen by the people during the Presi
dential campaign of 1916—based upon the slogan
"He kept us out of war"—might join in opposition
to the measure, or at least give it more careful con
sideration. But preventing a vote during the next
two days spelled only one word—filibuster!

George Norris, an advocate of a change in the
Senate rules to correct the abuses of filibustering
but feeling strongly that the issue of war itself was
at stake, adopted this very tactic "in spite of my
repugnance to the method." As parliamentary
floor leader for his group, he arranged speakers to
make certain that there was no possibility of a
break in the debate which would enable the bill
to come to a vote.

Day and night the debate continued; and on
the morning of March 4 the Senate was a scene
of weary disorder. "Those final minutes," Norris
later wrote, "live in my memory."

> In that chamber, men became slaves to emotion.
> The clash of anger and bitterness, in my judgment,
> never has been exceeded in the history of the
> United States. When the hour hand pointed to the
> arrival of noon, the chairman announced adjourn-
> ment. The filibuster had won. The conference report
> which would have authorized the arming of Amer-

ican ships had failed of Senate approval. . . . Tense
excitement prevailed throughout the entire country,
and especially in the Senate itself. . . . I have felt
from that day to this the filibuster was justified. I
never have apologized for the part I took in it. . . .
[We] honestly believed that, by our actions in that
struggle, we had averted American participation in
the war.

But theirs was a fleeting victory. For the President—in addition to immediately calling a special
session of Congress in which the Senate adopted
a closure rule to limit debate (with Norris' support)—also announced that a further examination
of the statutes had revealed that the executive
power already included the right to arm ships
without Congressional action. And the President
also let loose a blast, still frequently quoted today,
against "a little group of willful men, representing
no opinion but their own, that rendered the great
government of the United States helpless and contemptible."

It was believed in Washington that the conscience of the freshman from Nebraska had led
him, in the words of one Washingon corre-
spondent, to "his political death." The outraged
Nebraska State Legislature, with whooping en-

Because of his stand, Norris is shunned.

thusiasm, passed a resolution expressing the confidence of the state in President Wilson and his policies.

George Norris was saddened by the near unanimity with which "my own people condemned me . . . and asserted that I was misrepresenting my state." Although popularity was not his standard, he had tried, he later wrote, throughout his career "to do what in my own heart I believed to be right for the people at large." Thus, unwilling to "represent the people of Nebraska if they did not want me," he came to a dramatic decision—he would offer to resign from the Senate and submit to a special recall election, "to let my constituents decide whether I was representing them or misrepresenting them in Washington." In letters to the Governor and the Republican State Chairman, he urged a special election, agreeing to abide by the result and to waive whatever constitutional rights protected him from recall.

The Senator, announcing an open meeting in Lincoln to explain his position, was largely ignored by the press as he journeyed homeward. Attempting to get the Republican National Committeeman to act as chairman of the meeting, he was warned by that worthy gentleman that it was "not possible for this meeting to be held without trouble. I think the meeting will be broken up or at least you will have such an unfriendly audience that it will be impossible for you to make any coherent speech."

Unable to get a single friend or supporter to act as chairman, Norris was nevertheless determined to go through with the meeting. "I myself hired the hall," he told a lonely reporter in his deserted hotel room, "and it is to be my meeting. I am asking no one to stand sponsor for me or for my acts. But I have nothing to apologize for and nothing to take back."

Walking from his hotel to the city auditorium on a beautiful spring night, Norris anxiously noted that more than three thousand people—the concerned, the skeptical and the curious—had filled the auditorium, with many standing in the aisles and outside in the street. Calm but trembling, he walked out on the stage before them and stood for a moment without speaking, a solitary figure in a baggy black suit and a little shoestring tie. "I had expected an unfriendly audience," he wrote, "and it was with some fear that I stepped forward. When I entered the rear of the auditorium and stepped out on the stage, there was a deathlike silence. There was not a single handclap. But I had not expected applause; and I was delighted that I was not hissed."

In his homely, quiet, and yet intense manner, Senator Norris began with the simple phrase: "I have come home to tell you the truth."

> Immediately there was a burst of applause from all parts of the audience. Never in my lifetime has applause done me the good that did. . . . There was, in the hearts of the common people, a belief that underneath the deception and the misrepresentation, the political power and the influence, there was something artificial about the propaganda.

There was no violence, there was no heckling; and the tremendous crowd cheered mightily as Norris lashed out at his critics. His dry, simple but persistent language and the quiet intensity of his anger captivated his audience, as he insisted that their newspapers were not giving them the facts and that, despite warnings that he stay away until his role in the filibuster was forgotten, he wanted it to be remembered.

The crowd, after more than an hour, roared its approval. The newspapers were not so easily convinced or so willing to forgive. "His elaborate and ingenious explanation," said the *World Herald*, is "foolish nonsense . . . a silly statement, which has disgusted the people." "The Senator spent little time meeting the issue as it actually stood," said the *State Journal.* "He should not let his critics disturb his balance."

But Senator Norris, who was asked to appear before many groups to explain what he felt to be the true issues, met acclaim throughout the state; and the Governor having announced that he would not ask the Legislature to authorize a special recall election, the Senator returned to Washington better able to withstand the abuse which had not yet fully ceased.

During the next eleven years George Norris' fame and political fortune multiplied. In 1928, despite his continued differences with the Republican party and its administrations, the Nebraska Senator was one of the party's most prominent members, Chairman of the Senate Judiciary Committee and a potential Presidential nominee. But Norris himself scoffed at the latter reports:

> I have no expectation of being nominated for President. A man who has followed the political course I have is barred from the office. . . . I realize perfectly that no man holding the views I do is going to be nominated for the Presidency.

With an oath he rejected the suggestion that he accept a position as Herbert Hoover's running mate, and he attacked the Republican Convention's platform and the methods by which it had selected its nominees. In those years prior to the establishment of the T.V.A., the Senator from Nebraska was the nation's most outspoken advocate of public power; and he believed that the "monopolistic power trust" had dictated the nomination of Hoover and the Republican platform.

Unwilling to commit himself to the Democratic party he had always opposed, and whose platform he believed to be equally weak, Norris toured the country campaigning for fellow progressives regardless of party. But as the campaign utterances of Democratic nominee Al Smith of New York began to fall into line with Norris' own views, he was confronted with the most difficult political problem of his career.

George Norris was a Republican, a Midwesterner, a Protestant and a "dry," and Herbert Hoover was all of those things. But Al Smith—a Tammany Hall Democrat from the streets of New York, and a Catholic who favored the repeal of prohibition—was none of them. Surely Smith could have little support in Nebraska, which was also Republican, Midwestern, Protestant and dry by nature. Could Norris possibly desert his party, his state and his constituents under such circumstances?

He could. He had always maintained that he

"would like to abolish party responsibility and in its stead establish personal responsibility. Any man even though he be the strictest kind of Republican, who does not believe the things I stand for are right, should follow his convictions and vote against me." And thus in 1928 Norris finally declared that progressives

> had no place to land except in the Smith camp. . . . Shall we be so partisan that we will place our party above our country and refuse to follow the only leader who affords us any escape from the control of the [power] trust? . . . It seems to me we cannot crush our consciences and support somebody who we know in advance is opposed to the very things for which we have been fighting so many years.

But what about Smith's religious views? What about his attitude on the liquor question?

> It is possible for a man in public life to separate his religious beliefs from his political activities. . . . I am a Protestant and a dry, yet I would support a man who was a wet and a Catholic provided I believed he was sincerely in favor of law enforcement and was right on economic issues. . . . I'd rather trust an honest wet who is progressive and courageous in his makeup than politicians who profess to be on the dry side but do no more to make prohibition effective than all the rum runners and bootleggers in the country.

These were courageous sentiments, but they were lost on an indignant constituency.

The editor of the Walthill *Times* wrote: "I say it sadly, but I am through with Norris. Politically he is lost in the wilderness, far away from his old progressive friends."

"For a hungry farmer or a thirsty wet of less than average political judgment," said a Lincoln attorney who was close to the Norris camp, "there may be an excuse. But for a statesman of Norris' ability and experience there is no excuse."

But George Norris sought to help the hungry farmer even if it meant helping the thirsty wet. Unmoved by either appeals or attacks, he delivered a powerful plea for Smith at Omaha. The New York Governor, he said, had risen above the dictates of Tammany, while the techniques employed by the Republican Convention would "make Tammany Hall appear as a white-robed saint." He was "traveling in very distinguished company" by supporting the candidate of the opposing party, he told his audience, for Herbert Hoover himself had acted similarly ten years earlier. But for the most part his speech was an attack upon the power trust, "an octopus with slimy fingers that levies tribute upon every fireside," and upon Hoover's refusal to discuss these

questions: "to sin by silence when we should protest makes cowards out of men."

Finally, Norris closed his address by meeting
the religious issue openly:

> It is our duty as patriots to cast out this Un-
> American doctrine and rebuke those who have
> raised the torch of intolerance. All believers of any
> faith can unite and go forward in our political work
> to bring about the maximum amount of happiness
> for our people.

The landslide for Hoover, who carried practically every county and community in Nebraska,
as well as the country as a whole, embittered
Norris, who declared that Hoover had won on the
false questions of religion and prohibition, when
the real problems were power and farm relief. The
special interests and machine politicians, he said,
"kept this issue to the front [although] they knew
it was a false, wicked and unfair issue."

George Norris' filibuster against the Armed
Ship Bill had failed, both in its immediate goal of
preventing the President's action, and in its attempt to keep the nation out of the war into which
it was plunged a few months later. His campaign
for Al Smith also failed, and failed dismally. And
yet, as the Senator confided to a friend in later
years:

It happens very often that one tries to do something and fails. He feels discouraged, and yet he may discover years afterward that the very effort he made was the reason why somebody else took it up and succeeded. I really believe that whatever use I have been to progressive civilization has been accomplished in the things I failed to do than in the things I actually did do.

George Norris met with both success and failure in his long tenure in public office, stretching over nearly a half a century of American political life. But the essence of the man and his career was caught in a tribute paid to the Republican Senator from Nebraska by the Democratic Presidential nominee in September, 1932:

History asks, "Did the man have integrity?
Did the man have unselfishness?
Did the man have courage?
Did the man have consistency?"

There are few statesmen in America today who so definitely and clearly measure up to an affirmative answer to those four questions as does George W. Norris.

EIGHT

ROBERT A. TAFT

*"Liberty of the individual to think
his own thoughts."*

THE LATE SENATOR ROBERT A. TAFT of Ohio was
never President of the United States. Therein lies
his personal tragedy. And therein lies his national
greatness.

For the Presidency was a goal that Bob Taft
pursued throughout his career in the Senate, an
ambition that this son of a former President
always dreamed of realizing. As the leading ex-
ponent of the Republican philosophy for more
than a decade, "Mr. Republican" was bitterly disappointed by his failure on three different occasions even to receive the nomination.

But Robert A. Taft was also a man who stuck
fast to the basic principles in which he believed—
and when those fundamental principles were at
issue, not even the lure of the White House, or
the possibilities of injuring his candidacy, could
deter him from speaking out. He was an able politician, but on more than one occasion he chose to

speak out in defense of a position no politician with like ambitions would have endorsed. He was, moreover, a brilliant political analyst, who knew that during his lifetime the number of American voters who agreed with the fundamental tenets of his political philosophy was destined to be a permanent minority, and that only by flattering new blocs of support—while carefully refraining from alienating any group which contained potential Taft voters—could he ever hope to attain his goal. Yet he frequently flung to the winds the very restraints his own analysis advised, refusing to bow to any group, refusing to keep silent on any issue.

Perhaps we are as yet too close in time to the controversial elements in the career of Senator Taft to be able to measure his life with historical perspective. A man who can inspire intensely bitter enemies as well as intensely devoted followers is best judged after many years pass, enough years to permit the sediment of political and legislative battles to settle, so that we can assess our times more clearly.

But sufficient time has passed since 1946 to enable something of a detached view of Senator Taft's act of courage in that year. Unlike the acts of Daniel Webster or Edmund Ross, it did not

change history. Unlike those of John Quincy
Adams, or Thomas Benton, it did not bring about
his retirement from the Senate. Unlike most of
those deeds of courage previously described, it did
not even take place on the Senate floor. But as a
piece of sheer candor in a period when candor
was out of favor, as a bold plea for justice in a time
of intolerance and hostility, it is worth remembering here.

In October of 1946, Senator Robert A. Taft of
Ohio was the chief spokesman for the Republicans
in Washington, the champion of his party in the
national political arena and the likely Republican
nominee for the Presidency in 1948. It was a time
when even a Senator with such an established
reputation for speaking his mind would have
guarded his tongue, and particularly a Senator with
so much at stake as Bob Taft. The party which had
been his whole life, the Republicans of the Congress for whom he spoke, now once again were
nearing the brink of success in the fall elections.
Capturing for his party control of both Houses
of Congress would enhance Bob Taft's prestige,
reinforce his right to the Republican Presidential
nomination and pave the way for his triumphant
return to the White House from which his father
had been somewhat ungloriously ousted in 1912.

Or so it seemed to most political observers at the
time, who assumed the Republican leader would
say nothing to upset the applecart. With Congress
out of session, with the tide running strongly
against the incumbent Democrats, there appeared
to be no necessity for the Senator to make more
than the usual campaign utterances on the usual
issues.

But Senator Taft was disturbed—and when he
was disturbed it was his habit to speak out. He
was disturbed by the War Crimes Trials of Axis
leaders, then concluding in Germany and about
to commence in Japan. The Nuremberg Trials, in
which eleven notorious Nazis had been found
guilty under an impressively documented indict-
ment for "waging an aggressive war," had been
popular throughout the world and particularly in
the United States. Equally popular was the sentence already announced by the high tribunal:
death.

Still, why should he say anything? The Nuremberg Trials were at no time before the Congress
for consideration. They were not in any sense an
issue in the campaign. There was no Republican
or Democratic position on a matter enthusiasti-
cally applauded by the entire nation. And no
speech by any United States Senator, however

powerful, could prevent the death sentence from being carried out. To speak out unnecessarily would be politically costly and clearly futile.

But Bob Taft spoke out.

On October 6, 1946, Senator Taft appeared before a conference on our Anglo-American heritage, sponsored by Kenyon College in Ohio. The war crimes trial was not an issue upon which conference speakers were expected to comment. But titling his address "Equal Justice Under Law" Taft cast aside his general reluctance to embark upon startlingly novel and dramatic approaches. "The trial of the vanquished by the victors," he told an attentive if somewhat astonished audience, "cannot be impartial no matter how it is hedged about with the forms of justice."

> I question whether the hanging of those, who, however despicable, were the leaders of the German people, will ever discourage the making of aggressive war, for no one makes aggressive war unless he expects to win. About this whole judgment there is the spirit of vengeance, and vengeance is seldom justice. The hanging of the eleven men convicted will be a blot on the American record which we shall long regret.
>
> In these trials we have accepted the Russian idea of the purpose of trials—government policy and not justice—with little relation to Anglo-Saxon heritage.

Taft ponders the Nuremberg Trials.

By clothing policy in the forms of legal procedure, we may discredit the whole idea of justice in Europe for years to come. In the last analysis, even at the end of a frightful war, we should view the future with more hope if even our enemies believed that we had treated them justly in our English-speaking concept of law, in the provision of relief and in the final disposal of territory.

The speech exploded in the midst of a heated election campaign; and throughout the nation Republican candidates scurried for shelter while Democrats seized the opportunity to advance. Many, many people were outraged at Taft's remarks. Those who had fought, or whose men had fought and possibly died, to beat back the German aggressors were contemptuous of these fine phrases by a politician who had never seen battle. Those whose kinsmen or former countrymen had been among the Jews, Poles, Czechs and other nationality groups terrorized by Hitler and his cohorts were shocked. The memories of the gas chambers at Buchenwald and other Nazi concentration camps, the stories of hideous atrocities which had been refreshed with new illustrations at Nuremberg, and the anguish and suffering which each new military casualty list had brought to thousands of American homes—these were

among the immeasurable influences which caused
many to react with pain and indignation when
a United States Senator deplored the trials and
sentences of these merely "despicable" men.

Even in the nation's Capital, where Taft was
greatly admired and his blunt candor was more
or less expected, the reaction was no different.
G.O.P. leaders generally declined official comment, but privately expressed their fears over the
consequences for their Congressional candidates.
At a press conference, the Chairman of the Republican Congressional Campaign Committee refused to comment on the subject, stating that he
had "his own ideas" on the Nuremberg Trials but
did not "wish to enter into a controversy with
Senator Taft."

Senator Taft was disheartened by the voracity
of his critics—and extremely uncomfortable when
one of the acquitted Nazi leaders, Franz Von
Papen, told interviewers upon his release from
prison that he agreed with Taft's speech. A spokesman for Taft issued only one terse statement: "He
has stated his feelings on the matter and feels
that if others want to criticize him, let them go
ahead." But the Ohio Senator could not understand why even his old supporter, newspaper
columnist David Lawrence, called his position

nothing more than a "technical quibble." And he must have been particularly distressed when respected Constitutional authorities such as the President of the American Bar Association, the Chairman of its Executive Committee and other leading members of the legal profession all deplored his statement and defended the trials as being in accordance with international law.

For Robert Taft had spoken, not in "defense of the Nazi murderers" (as a labor leader charged), not in defense of isolationism (as most observers assumed), but in defense of what he regarded to be the traditional American concepts of law and justice. As the apostle of strict constitutionalism, as the chief defense attorney for the conservative way of life and government, Robert Alphonso Taft was undeterred by the possibilities of injury to his party's precarious position or his own Presidential prospects. To him, justice was at stake, and all other concerns were trivial. "It illustrates at once," a columnist observed at that time, "the extreme stubbornness, integrity and political strongheadedness of Senator Taft."

The storm raised by his speech eventually died down. It did not, after all the uproar, appear to affect the Republican sweep in 1946, nor was it—at least openly—an issue in Taft's drive for the

Presidential nomination in 1948. The Nazi leaders were hanged, and Taft and the country went on to other matters. But we are not concerned today with the question of whether Taft was right or wrong in his condemnation of the Nuremberg Trials. What is noteworthy is the illustration furnished by this speech of Taft's unhesitating courage in standing against the flow of public opinion for a cause he believed to be right. His action was characteristic of the man who was labeled a reactionary, who was proud to be a conservative and who authored these lasting definitions of liberalism and liberty:

> Liberalism implies particularly freedom of thought, freedom from orthodox dogma, the right of others to think differently from one's self. It implies a free mind, open to new ideas and willing to give attentive consideration. . . .
>
> When I say liberty, I mean liberty of the individual to think his own thoughts and live his own life as he desires to think and live.

This was the creed by which Senator Taft lived, and he sought in his own fashion and in his own way to provide an atmosphere in America in which others could do likewise.

THE MEANING OF COURAGE

THIS HAS BEEN a book about courage and politics. Politics furnished the situations, courage provided the theme. Courage, the universal virtue, is comprehended by us all—but these portraits of courage do not dispel the mysteries of politics.

For not a single one of the men whose stories appear in the preceding pages offers a simple, clear-cut picture of motivation and accomplishment. In each of them complexities, inconsistencies and doubts arise to plague us. However detailed may have been our study of his life, each man remains something of an enigma. However clear the effect of his courage, the cause is shadowed by a veil which cannot be torn away. We may confidently state the reasons why—yet something always seems to elude us. We think we hold the answer in our hands—yet somehow it slips through our fingers.

Motivation, as any psychiatrist will tell us, is always difficult to assess. It is particularly difficult to trace in the murky sea of politics. Those who abandoned their state and section for the national interest—men like Daniel Webster and Sam Houston, whose ambitions for higher office could not be hidden—laid themselves open to the charge that they sought only to satisfy their ambition for the Presidency. Those who broke with their party to fight for broader principles—men like John Quincy Adams and Edmund Ross—faced the accusation that they accepted office under one banner and yet deserted it in a moment of crisis for another.

But in the particular events set forth in the preceding chapters, I am persuaded after long study of the record that the national interest, rather than private or political gain, furnished the basic motivation for the actions of those whose deeds are therein described. This does not mean that many of them did not seek, though rarely with success, to wring advantage out of the difficult course they had adopted. For as politicians—and it is surely no disparagement to term all of them politicians—they were clearly justified in doing so.

Of course, the acts of courage described in this book would be more inspiring and would shine more with the traditional luster of hero-worship if we assumed that each man forgot wholly about himself in his dedication to higher principles. But it may be that President John Adams, surely as disinterested as well as wise a public servant as we ever had, came much nearer to the truth when he wrote in his *Defence of the Constitutions . . . of the United States:* "It is not true, in fact, that any people ever existed who love the public better than themselves."

If this be true, what then caused the statesmen mentioned in the preceding pages to act as they did? It was not because they "loved the public better than themselves." On the contrary it was precisely because they did *love themselves*—because each one's need to maintain his own respect for himself was more important to him than his popularity with others—because his desire to win or maintain a reputation for integrity and courage was stronger than his desire to maintain his office —because his conscience, his personal standard of ethics, his integrity or morality, call it what you will—was stronger than the pressures of public disapproval—because his faith that *his* course was the best one, and would ultimately be vindicated, outweighed his fear of public reprisal.

The meaning of courage, like political motivations, is frequently misunderstood. Some enjoy the excitement of its battles, but fail to note the implications of its consequences. Some admire its virtues in other men and other times, but fail to comprehend its current potentialities. Perhaps, to make clearer the significance of these stories of political courage, it would be well to say what this book is not.

It is not intended to justify independence for the sake of independence, obstinacy to all compromise or excessively proud and stubborn adherence to one's own personal convictions. It is not intended to suggest that there is, on every issue, one right side and one wrong side, and that all Senators except those who are knaves or fools will find the right side and stick to it. On the contrary, I share the feelings expressed by Prime Minister Melbourne, who, when irritated by the criticism of the then youthful historian T. B. Macaulay, remarked that he would like to be as sure of anything as Macaulay seemed to be of everything. And nine years in Congress have taught me the wisdom of Lincoln's words: "There are few things wholly evil or wholly good. Almost everything, especially of Government policy, is an inseparable compound of the two, so that our best judgment of the preponderance between them is continually demanded."

This book is not intended to suggest that party regularity and party responsibility are necessary

evils which should at no time influence our decisions. It is not intended to suggest that the local
interests of one's state or region have no legitimate
right to consideration at any time. On the contrary,
the loyalties of every Senator are distributed
among his party, his state and section, his country
and his conscience. On party issues, his party
loyalties are normally controlling. In regional dis-
putes, his regional responsibilities will likely guide
his course. It is on national issues, on matters of
conscience which challenge party and regional
loyalties, that the test of courage is presented.

It may take courage to battle one's President,
one's party or the overwhelming sentiment of one's
nation; but these do not compare, it seems to me,
to the courage required of the Senator defying the
angry power of the very constituents who control
his future. It is for this reason that I have not included in this work the stories of this nation's most
famous "insurgents"—John Randolph, Thaddeus
Stevens, Robert La Follette and all the rest—men
of courage and integrity, but men whose battles
were fought with the knowledge that they enjoyed
the support of the voters back home.

Finally, this book is not intended to disparage
democratic government and popular rule. The
examples of constituent passions unfairly condemn-

ing a man of principle are not unanswerable arguments against permitting the widest participation in the electoral process. The stories of men who accomplished good in the face of cruel calumnies from the public are not final proof that we should at all times ignore the feelings of the voters on national issues. For, as Winston Churchill has said, "Democracy is the worst form of government—except all those other forms that have been tried from time to time." We can improve our democratic processes, we can enlighten our understanding of its problems, and we can increase our respect for those men of integrity who find it necessary, from time to time, to act contrary to public opinion. But we cannot solve the problems of legislative independence and responsibility by abolishing or curtailing democracy.

For democracy means much more than popular government and majority rule, much more than a system of political techniques to flatter or deceive powerful blocs of voters. A democracy that has no George Norris to point to—no monument of individual conscience in a sea of popular rule—is not worthy to bear the name. The true democracy, living and growing and inspiring, puts its faith in the people—faith that the people will not simply elect men who will represent their views ably and faithfully, but also elect men who will exercise their conscientious judgment—faith that the people will not condemn those whose devotion to principle leads them to unpopular courses, but will reward courage, respect honor and ultimately recognize right.

These stories are the stories of such a democracy. Indeed, there would be no such stories had this nation not maintained its heritage of free speech and dissent, had it not fostered honest conflicts of opinion, had it not encouraged tolerance for unpopular views. Cynics may point to our inability to provide a happy ending for each chapter. But I am certain that these stories will not be looked upon as warnings to beware of being courageous. For the continued political success of many of those who withstood the pressures of public opinion, and the ultimate vindication of the rest, enables us to maintain our faith in the long-run judgment of the people.

And thus neither the demonstrations of past courage nor the need for future courage are confined to the Senate alone. Not only do the problems of courage and conscience concern every officeholder in our land, however humble or mighty, and to whomever he may be responsible—voters, a legislature, a political machine or a party organization. They concern as well every voter in our land—and they concern those who do not vote, those who take no interest in Government, those who have only disdain for the politician and his profession. They concern everyone who has ever complained about corruption in high places, and everyone who has ever insisted that his representative abide by his wishes. For, in a democracy, every citizen, regardless of his interest in politics, "holds office"; every one of us is in a position of responsibility; and, in the final analysis, the kind of government we get depends upon how we fulfill those responsibilities. We, the people, are the boss, and we will get the kind of political leadership, be it good or bad, that we demand and deserve.

These problems do not even concern politics alone—for the same basic choice of courage or compliance continually faces us all, whether we fear the anger of constituents, friends, a board of directors or our union, whenever we stand against the flow of opinion on strongly contested issues. For without belittling the courage with which men have died, we should not forget those acts of courage with which men—such as the subjects of this book—have *lived*. The courage of life is often a less dramatic spectacle than the courage of a final moment; but it is no less a magnificent mixture of triumph and tragedy. A man does what he must —in spite of personal consequences, in spite of obstacles and dangers and pressures—and that is the basis of all human morality.

To be courageous, these stories make clear, requires no exceptional qualifications, no magic formula, no special combination of time, place and circumstance. It is an opportunity that sooner or later is presented to us all. Politics merely furnishes one arena which imposes special tests of courage. In whatever arena of life one may meet the challenge of courage, whatever may be the sacrifices he faces if he follows his conscience—the loss of his friends, his fortune, his contentment, even the esteem of his fellow men—each man must decide for himself the course he will follow. The stories of past courage can define that ingredient—they can teach, they can offer hope, they can provide inspiration. But they cannot supply courage itself. For this each man must look into his own soul.

(mem. ed.)

J
920
K

Kennedy
Profiles in courage

Date Due

FEB 6		
DEC 8		
AN 5		
MAR		
AP		

(mem. ed.)

J
920
K

Kennedy
Profiles in
courage

FEB 6 '69	1884	AUG 0 3 2004	ren
DEC 8 '71	1702		
JAN 5 '72	1951		
MAR 29 '72	2327		
APR 24 '73	3461		